TERMITES: A STUDY IN SOCIAL BEHAVIOUR

*

Biological Sciences

Editor

PROFESSOR A. J. CAIN
MA, D.PHIL
Professor of Zoology
in the University of Liverpool

Nest of *Macrotermes natalensis* in vertical section. (Reproduced by permission of P.-P. Grassé.)

TERMITES: A STUDY IN SOCIAL BEHAVIOUR

P. E. Howse

Lecturer in Zoology at
the University of Southampton

HUTCHINSON UNIVERSITY LIBRARY
LONDON

HUTCHINSON & CO *(Publishers)* LTD
178–202 Great Portland Street, London W1

London Melbourne Sydney
Auckland Bombay Toronto
Johannesburg New York

First published 1970

*The cover design of the paperback edition shows
part of a figure from Smeathman's account of
Termites, published in 1781*

*This book has been set in Times, printed in Great Britain
on Smooth Wove paper by Anchor Press, and
bound by Wm. Brendon, both of Tiptree, Essex*

09 100841 7 (paper)
09 100840 9 (cased)

. . . when we come to consider the wonderful order of these insects, and of their subterraneous cities, they will appear foremost on the list of the wonders of the creation.

H. SMEATHMAN, 1781

CONTENTS

PLATES

FIGURES

PREFACE

This book is about the behaviour of termites and some of the fundamental aspects of their society. It is not an exhaustive review, and therefore I hope that some of the termitologists I know will not be offended if I seem to have capriciously disregarded some of their publications.

Many undergraduates today appear to learn little more of termites than their symbiosis with protozoa (which is not, in any case, general). Also, textbooks of entomology still appear in which the section on termites could well have been written thirty years ago. The deficiencies have arisen because a great amount of research on the biology of termites has been published in French and German, and often in journals that are not commonly found in this country. The few books on termites that have been published in recent years have been primarily concerned with termites as pests, and one book which will complement this one admirably in this respect is *Termites, their recognition and control* by Dr W. V. Harris (Longmans, 1961).

I am very grateful to Dr M. F. Claridge, Dr J. D. Carthy and Professor Martin Lüscher for reading some of the chapters in manuscript and for making a number of helpful suggestions. I am also indebted to Mrs Pat Wagner, who has drawn many of the figures, and to Mr John Baynham, who has done the photographic work for me. Dr W. V. Harris of the Colonial Termite Research Unit, London, has been most helpful to me in a number of ways, not the least of which was to interest me in termites for the first time ten years ago. Professor P.-P. Grassé, Dr E. Ernst, Mme Paulette Bodot, and Dr J. E. Ruelle have kindly allowed me

to reproduce photographs that are theirs, and Dr M. J. Delany
has helped me by reading some chapters in proof. For permission
to quote from a poem by Ogden Nash on p. 17 I am grateful to
the author and Messrs. J. M. Dent & Sons Ltd.

I

THE HABITS AND IMPORTANCE OF TERMITES

Some of the early explorers made reference to the white ants they saw in the tropics, which built mound-like dwellings for themselves. The mounds were said to be so firm that even elephants or heavily laden wagons could make no impression on them. A traveller in Senegal said that the mounds were often so numerous and large that, at a distance, they were easily mistaken for native village huts.

The first detailed account of termites was given to the Royal Society of London in 1781 by Henry Smeathman[152] who had returned from a voyage to Guinea. It was said that his paper was received with some scepticism, which is scarcely surprising, for he described small insects that could build towers standing well above the height of a man. A tower contained nurseries, provision chambers, guard-rooms, corridors, bridges, subterranean streets, canals, and a royal palace. Among the versatile insects were civilians, chemists, water-diviners, well-borers, architects, engineers and surveyors. We may think today that Smeathman was excessively free with his imagination, and so he was, but this was because he interpreted what he saw in terms of the only other society he knew—human society. It was well over a century later before enough was known about insect societies for it to be realised that they are fundamentally different from our own and for descriptions that were not anthropomorphic to become possible.

Much to the distress of entomologists, 'white ants' is, in many languages the common name for termites. It is quite

[152] Superior figures refer to bibliographical references at the end of the book.

true that in their habits termites show more similarities to ants than to any other insects, but in other features they have great affinities with cockroaches, and it has even been suggested that they should be placed in the same order as cockroaches. They are, however, placed in a separate order of their own, the Isoptera, widely separated from the Hymenoptera which contains the only other true social insects: the bees, wasps and ants.

There are a number of easily recognisable differences between ants and termites. The colour of ants is generally much darker as a result of their much thicker and harder cuticle. Unlike termites, ants have a very slender 'waist', and may carry a sting at the end of the abdomen. A very fundamental difference between ants and termites lies in their development. In termites, as in cockroaches, the development is direct; that is, something like a miniature adult hatches from the egg. This individual moults at intervals, gradually increases in size, and acquires wing-pads which get larger at each moult. The development of ants (and other Hymenoptera) is indirect: the egg hatches into a grub or larva which is very unlike the adult and after a series of moults this transforms into a quiescent pupa from which the adult emerges in due course. Therefore in the Hymenoptera the adults are the functional elements of the society whereas in the termites immature forms comprise virtually the whole of the society.

Social insects differ from others in that one or both of the parents live together under a common shelter with colonies of their offspring. The behaviour of the individuals is coordinated, so that cooperative activities like foraging and nest-building are possible. This is helped by a certain degree of division of labour: different castes of individuals are present, each specialised for particular functions. In termite societies these are workers, soldiers, and reproductive forms of various kinds (Plate II). Adult reproductives are found in the colony only at certain times of the year; they are the winged forms that leave and found new colonies. Soldiers are the defensive elements of the society, workers undertake the everyday activities of gathering food, building and so on.

Compared with honeybees, for example, there has been relatively little research into the biology of termites. This is undoubtedly because of their geographical distribution, which overlaps very little with European and North American centres of research. They are predominantly creatures of tropical regions, and the 9·5°C annual isotherm of both hemispheres encloses almost all the two to three thousand known species. Only a few species are found in Europe, but they do not extend as far north as Britain. One species, *Kalotermes flavicollis,* is common in southern France where it causes damage to vine stocks, and it has been used extensively in research. The other species found in southern Europe is *Reticulitermes lucifugus.* In addition, a variety of this species was apparently introduced in the region of La Rochelle in ships' timbers. The insects went for a long time undetected, but in 1797 it was found that they had ruined stores of stacked oak for making warships, and in 1820 Napoleon's ship, *Le Génois,* had to be broken up because of the damage done by termites. A North American species, *Reticulitermes flavipes,* was introduced into Hamburg about thirty years ago. A subterranean species with a predilection for moist conditions, it survived in spite of the low temperatures above ground.

Many more species are found in North America, but most of these, like the European species, are wood-boring. Their behaviour tends to be rather dull compared with many of the tropical species. They are also regarded as primitive, because termites that have been found in amber are often closely related species. The most primitive of living species is held to be *Mastotermes darwiniensis,* which is found north of the tropic of Capricorn in Australia. Members of the same family, the Mastotermitidae, are known as Tertiary fossils, mostly from southern England and Europe. *M. darwiniensis* is the only living member of this family. It has, uniquely among living termites, an anal lobe to its hind wings like that of cockroaches, and its eggs are laid in a double row and cemented together, a feature very reminiscent of cockroaches.

Termites are probably best known as destroyers of wood; and this is true of *M. darwiniensis.* Three of the other five families of termites, the dry-wood termites (*Kalotermitidae*), damp-wood termites (*Termopsidae*) and subterranean termites (*Rhinotermitidae*), eat wood. According to Ogden Nash:

> Some primal termite knocked on wood
> And tasted it, and found it good,
> And that is why your Cousin May
> Fell through the parlour floor today

But it was obviously not quite as simple as that, because termites by themselves cannot digest cellulose. Symbiotic protozoa, which are harboured in special sections of their intestines, perform the digestion of cellulose for many species. It is very likely that such protozoa were present in the cockroach-like ancestors of termites. There is a 'missing link' in the form of a wood-eating cockroach, *Cryptocercus punctulatus,* which is found in the Appalachian mountains in the eastern USA. This insect digests cellulose with the aid of flagellate protozoa, and two of the genera it harbours are also found in termites.[25] It is, moreover, semisocial, living in small colonies in damp wood. Other cockroaches have bacteria as symbionts, which are contained in their fat bodies and play some role in nutrition, but they have no flagellates, perhaps having lost them during the course of evolution. *M. darwiniensis* has both intestinal flagellates and intracellular bacteria: another feature which is seized upon by those who accuse it of primitiveness.

The view that *Mastotermes* and the dry-wood termites are primitive is in many ways an unfortunate one. They share certain morphological features with fossil species. How their behaviour has changed we shall never know, but it is often elaborate and exquisitely adapted to their way of life. Colonies numbering millions of individuals have been reported for *M. darwiniensis,*[78] and galleries of the nest may extend for large distances underground to timber or plants on which the termites feed. *Kalotermes minor* burrows into the extremely hard wood of the Monterey cedars that line the Californian coast. Yet when these trees die they do not rot, but stand like twisted stone monuments and an axe will scarcely scratch the surface of the wood. *Neotermes tectonae,* found in the East Indies, burrows into teak. Insects such as these are so successful at making a living, avoiding predation and disseminating their kind that they are a menace to the buildings and constructions of man.

The family *Hodotermitidae* comprises the Harvester termites. These forage in columns above-ground for grasses, which are cut into short lengths and transported back to the nest. These termites are usually active by day, have distinct pigmented compound eyes, and may have a generally darker coloration than other species. They depend upon flagellates for the digestion of the cellulose in their diet.

The remaining family, the *Termitidae,* contains about three-quarters of all the known species, varying considerably in their habits. Nests may be arboreal (*Nasutitermes*), in the form of large mounds (*Macrotermes, Amitermes*), or entirely subterranean (*Apicotermes*). Members of this family are sometimes referred to as the 'higher' termites because of their greater specialisations for social life. They do not have symbiotic protozoa, but rely on a rich microflora of bacteria, contained in the posterior regions of the intestine, for the digestion of cellulose. Some species have, in addition to the bacteria, amoebae or ciliates which may play a role in the digestion of cellulose. The *Macrotermitinae*, an important sub-family, have developed a symbiotic association with fungi of the genus *Termitomyces*. These grow inside the nest on 'fungus gardens' which are composed of faecal material. The fungi attack the lignin in this and break it down to simpler substances which the termites (and their bacteria) can digest[62]. The fungi themselves also appear to have favourable effects on the growth and survival of the termites.

It is thought that the intestinal flora and fauna which are essential for the nutrition of termites were key factors in the evolution of termite social life. Social life (*sensu stricto*) in insects is attained when the young are not only protected and fed by the parent but take part in rearing additional broods. Stages intermediate to this condition may be seen in a variety of insect species. It seems likely that the early termites lived together in groups as a result of a tendency to burrow in decaying wood and squeeze into narrow spaces. Then, they probably developed a tendency to feed on each other's faeces, as these might still contain a proportion of undigested cellulose. The results would have been twofold: firstly, intestinal symbionts would have been transmitted rapidly throughout the group, and secondly, trophallaxis—mutual feeding, licking and grooming—would have been facilitated.

There is no doubt that trophallaxis is of immense importance to the structure and cohesion of insect societies. Young wasps, ants, and termites produce secretions which are attractive to the adults which respond by feeding the young. The newly hatched termites are thus provided with a ready supply of easily digested food in the form of secretions or excretions. The larvae of wasps produce a sugary secretion from their labial glands, which, in addition to stimulating trophallaxis with the adults, also provides the latter with a reserve of food at times of shortage.[120] Honeybee larvae do not, apparently, produce an attractive secretion, but the workers feed them with a highly nutritive 'royal jelly', which is a secretion of the salivary glands, for a few days after hatching.

Food brought into the nest is rapidly distributed to all members of the colony by trophallactic activity and, with it, special secretions that may have important biological effects. An example is the 'queen substance' produced by the mandibular glands of the queen honeybee. This is spread over her body when she grooms herself and so becomes available to the workers who lick and groom her. The substance is kept in circulation around the colony by trophallaxis and inhibits the development of the ovaries of the workers and prevents the rearing of further queens.[22] There is little doubt that chemicals concerned in regulating the development of castes in termites are also rapidly distributed throughout the colony by trophallaxis, but the origin of the secretions is not known.

Trophallaxis also helps to ensure that all members of a colony smell (or taste) the same, and this means that intruders to the nest can be recognised quickly.

Termite colonies, however large, generally have only one parent couple: the king and queen, which are the founders of the colony. In species which develop very large colonies the queen tends to a very large abdomen, an adaptation for the continuous production of large numbers of eggs. This obesity is known in the entomological world as *physogastry*, and it is not marked in termites that live in wood, where it would obviously be disadvantageous since the colony is not static in position and has to move when the wood is eaten out. Physogastry is most marked in the mound-building termites, where the king and queen are confined in a thick-walled 'queen cell' in the heart of the nest. The queen of *Macrotermes natalensis* has been known to increase her length from 35 mm to 140 mm as a result of hypertrophy of the abdomen, increasing her weight 125 times in the process.[16] It has been reported that the queen of *Odontotermes badius* lays eggs at the rate of 4,000 a day, which would result in 1,460,000 in a year. The queen of *M. natalensis* can produce 36,000 eggs in a day which amounts to one every two seconds (on average) or 13,000,000 in a year.[76] In view of their impressive fecundity, it is scarcely surprising to find that queens are highly prized as aphrodisiacs in many countries throughout the tropics. They are said to be used by Hindus for restoring the lost powers of the elders, but in certain regions of the Congo they are eaten only by the women; if they are eaten by men, this is believed to result in a loss of generative powers. The general medicinal properties of the queens are, however, not completely open to doubt, since an anti-microbial substance has been isolated from the queen of *Odontotermes redemanni*.

Nothing is known of the age to which a queen normally lives, but it is known that mounds can exist for great lengths of time. Skaife[151] has estimated the age of the relatively small mounds of *Amitermes atlanticus* as thirty to fifty years. In 1872 Hill[79] damaged the top of a large nest of the Australian species *Nasutitermes triodiae*. He identified it sixty-three years later and found it still to be active. The record for longevity appears to be held by a mound in Southern Rhodesia in which was an iron-age burial mound found to be about 700 years old.[161] Skeletons were preserved in the alkaline soil of the mound, whereas bones buried in the acid soil around the mound were destroyed within a period of about twenty years. Only a small portion of the original mound was occupied by termites, which could not, of course, have been descendants of the original colony.

A feature that almost all organisms have in common is the possession of a rhythm of activity within a period of about twenty-four hours. Such rhythms were once called *diurnal*, but this term is ambiguous because it might be taken to suggest that the peak of activity is during the daytime, and has been replaced by the term *circadian*, which means 'about a day'. Circadian rhythms of activity were found by Andrews and Middleton[4] in colonies of *Nasutitermes costalis*, a tree-nesting species found around Montego Bay. They put glass 'windows' into two covered galleries running from a tree nest down to the trunk of a palm tree. The windows had to be continually renewed because it took the termites only thirty-five to fifty minutes to occlude the glass with their faecal building material, but it was found that more termites were entering the nest than leaving it during the daytime, with the reverse situation at night. The study was completed on a nest which was taken indoors, hung from a ceiling and connected to food and water by long sticks. The greatest foraging activity occurred from 1 am to 5 am and the least from 1 pm to 5 pm when it was reduced by about 80%.

Using different techniques of research, similar circadian rhythms of activity have been found in species of *Cubitermes* in the Congo. Nests of *C. sankurensis* were collected at different times of the day and night and found to contain the greatest

numbers of termites at 1 pm and the smallest numbers at 1 am.[15]
C. exiguus[121] was found to show a cyclic repletion of the gut,
which was relatively full at 4 am and relatively empty at 6 pm

There is no reason to think that activity patterns of this nature
are not general. There is a particular advantage to termites in
foraging at night, because the relative humidity is likely to rise
as the temperature falls. Water loss through the thin cuticle of
the insects is then minimised. *Trinervitermes carbonarius,* a
west African snouted harvester termite, forages at night, coming
out in the open air some distance from the nest, but only when the
temperature is relatively stable and the relative humidity is close
to 94%.[12] The foraging activity fluctuates throughout the year.
It is the highest in the rainy season and lowest at the beginning
of the dry season (Fig. 1*a*). These termites live in savanna areas
which can become very dry, but their seasonal rhythm of activity
ensures that they collect the grasses they feed upon when their
nutritive value is highest. The cut grasses are restored as reserves
which are used during the dry season.

Mounds of *Macrotermes natalensis* also occur in savanna areas.
These termites also collect grasses, but under the cover of earthen
tubes that they build over the stems. The material they collect is
stored in chambers in the nest and is incorporated into the fungus
gardens. This incorporation takes place within forty-eight hours,
and the fungus invades new gardens within a similar period after
this. The foraging activity of this species is continuous and
fluctuates less in accordance with the climatic changes than it
does in *T. carbonarius* (Fig. 1*b*). The reason for this difference
apparently lies in the ability of *Macrotermes* workers to construct
galleries down to the water table. They are thus relatively free
from the dangers of desiccation during the dry season. The peak
of the foraging activity of both species actually coincides with
the period of light rains, which is also the time when the nymphs
that moult to the winged forms appear in the nest.

The flights of termites are more or less precisely timed annual
events, and will be discussed in more detail in a later chapter.
In many tropical species they take place near the beginning of the
heavy rains. It seems that the onset of the rains may provide a
cue for synchronous emergence of a species over a wide area and
that the enhanced growth of vegetation during the season will
present conditions favourable for rebuilding depleted colonies
and for creating new ones.

A further activity in some species which varies in relation to the cycle of rainfall is that of nest-building. In *Trinervitermes carbonarius* and two other species which construct small mound nests in the Ivory Coast (*Amitermes evuncifer* and *Cubitermes*

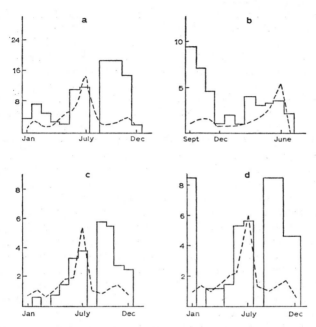

Fig. 1 (a) Seasonal variations in the foraging activity of (*a*) *Trinervitermes carbonarius*, and (*b*) *Macrotermes natalensis* in the Ivory Coast.

The cycle of building activity by (*c*) *Trinervitermes carbonarius*, and (*d*) *Macrotermes natalensis* in 1963.

The ordinates in the graphs are activity indices and the dotted lines indicate the cycle of rainfall (after Bodot[12]).

severus), the cycle of building follows the amount of rainfall very closely (Fig. 1c), but in *Macrotermes natalensis* the relationship is rather obscure (Fig. 1d). It appears that the building activity is highly dependent upon a supply of moisture, which must be present in the superficial layers of the soil for the first three species, although *M. natalensis* can obtain water from the water table. Observations on this species in the Congo have shown that the building activity is highest at the beginning of the rainy season and that this appears to be an adaptation to prevent rain from soaking into the mound, since the building decreases the porosity of the outer wall.[140]

Naturally, the different behaviour of species that live in the same area will tend to reduce the competition between them and make co-existence possible. A neat illustration of this is provided by a study made by Sands[142] on five species of *Trinervitermes* in northern Nigeria: *ebenerianus, carbonarius, suspensus, oeconomus* and *auriterrae*. The first three species harvest and store grass fragments inside the nest. The last two do not store them, and this means that they must forage continuously and that they are therefore more suited to living in sheltered sites rather than the open savanna where grass fires preclude foraging at certain times of year. The species that live more in the open savanna may also benefit from the insulation provided against the heat of the sun by the grasses which are stored near the surface of the mound. These species are also more darkly pigmented.

T. ebenerianus forages most actively and tends to take coarser grasses than *suspensus*. *T. carbonarius* makes mud pathways, as does *auriterrae*, but the latter is the only species to build pathways up trees. *T. oeconomus* does not form foraging columns like the others, but browses on rotting leaves and dry grass. *T. carbonarius* appears, on the whole, to be better adapted to conditions in southern Guinea, since the young colonies develop faster in this species and begin to forage when precipitation there is relatively mild. Rain is very heavy at the same time in the northern savanna and would tend to flood young colonies.[143]

Strong aggressive responses have been found between members of different colonies of a species of harvester termites in South Africa. By observing these responses it was possible to show that colonies of *Hodotermes mossambicus* had a territory of about 93 m squared. When the termites met with those of another species living in the same area they 'preferred to avoid each other rather than to fight'.[128]

Aggression in termites, as in other social insects, appears to be released if one individual meets another that does not have the same 'colony odour'. There is evidence that the cuticle is capable of adsorbing certain substances. Some of these may depend, for example, on the particular sort of food the insects have been exploiting, so that all members of the colony carry the same 'badge of identification', which is distributed around the colony by trophallactic activity. The efficiency of trophallaxis in distributing substances is shown by experiments in which workers of *Cubitermes fungifaber* were given humus to eat containing radioactive phosphorous. This could be detected in the colony after four hours, and in the saliva of most of the workers after twenty-five to thirty hours.[1]

In *Hodotermes mossambicus* the colony odour is lost equally rapidly: there are strong aggressive responses among nest mates that have been isolated for a day. On the other hand, Andrews,[3] who made a study of *Nasutitermes rippertii* in Jamaica, found that nest mates could be returned to the nest after a separation of hours or days without being attacked. He found different degrees of hostility among the individuals of different colonies, but discovered that this could be eliminated if foreign termites were first washed with a watery extract of the potential host colony. Emerson succeeded in mixing two initially inimicable colonies of *Nasutitermes guayanae* by first shaking up one with nest material of the other. It appears, then, that the colony odour acts by fatiguing the chemoreceptive sense organs of termites so that they can respond only to substances that are chemically different. It is very likely that the termite cuticle carries its own secretions which release aggression but are masked by the colony odour. Individuals of *Zootermopsis angusticollis* will react very strongly to contact with the cuticle of other insects (e.g. cockroaches) but show no response to earthworm cuticle, human skin or cuticle from the larva of a flour beetle. This suggests that the insects that termites accept as 'guests' in their nests may be tolerated because of their lack of 'insect odour' rather than because they have the 'colony odour'.[88]

Economic importance

Evidence has come to light in recent years which shows that termites have had an enormous effect on the landscape of large areas in Africa. This applies mainly to the mound-building termites of the genus *Macrotermes*. The mounds of *M. bellicosus* may reach a diameter of 30 m and a height of 6 m. These mounds and those of *M. natalensis*, which are somewhat smaller occur in large numbers at a density of up to 2·9 per hectare,[15] giving a very peculiar character to the landscape. These two species, and also *M. goliath* are inhabitants of the savanna. When forest land is cleared they colonise it and later die off if the forest re-invades. Abandoned mounds in the savanna are rapidly colonised by vegetation; they have a higher mineral content than the surrounding soils, are better drained, and are less affected by grass fires because of their height. The colonisation begins with grasses and is followed by trees, resulting in islands of woodland in grassland: a so-called termite savanna. These islands eventually spread and coalesce to form continuous forest.[74]

While some species of termites can cause extensive damage to crops in tropical regions, it appears that others perform a valuable function in increasing the aeration and drainage of the soil. Sands[142] concludes that 'the widespread use of even minute doses of persistent chlorinated hydrocarbon insecticides (on savanna soils) could greatly reduce termite populations, with the possible consequences of further degradation and erosion of already infertile compacted soils'. There is also evidence that the mound-builders may be responsible for the re-establishment of new soils in some areas after erosion has taken place. In some regions of the Congo and Uganda 'stone lines' have been found in the subsoil, which appear to have been exposed through soil erosion in the quaternary period.[32] It is believed that the first stage in the formation of the sand and clay soil lying above the stones was the colonisation of the area by *Macrotermes* species which became active as the rainfall increased. In building, *Macrotermes* workers tend to bring up clay particles from near the water table Their mounds therefore tend to be rich in mineral salts, and, as a result of their use of faeces in building, rich in organic material. The existence of certain sand and clay soils in east central Brazil has also been attributed to the action of mound-building termites. The termites that exist there today build rather steep-sided mounds and these do not have the same influence on the vegetation that the low domed *Macrotermes* mounds do in Africa. Instead, the latter are represented by fungus-growing ants which build mounds of a similar shape.

It is neither within the scope of this book, nor the competence of the author, to discuss at length the importance of termites as pests or the measures used to control them, but their effects are widespread and extremely costly. It is said that our knowledge of the history of South America has been severely impoverished by termites, which have eaten most of the books more than a century old. Most species have a strong aversion to contact with the outside air, no doubt based on their sensitivity to light and minute air movements. Hence their presence may go undetected until the structure that they are inhabiting suddenly collapses. Subterranean termites have been known to make tubular galleries up to the second story of a house, where they attacked a box of candles. They have also been admired for a habit of eating the corks of stored wine bottles while leaving a thin layer of cork which prevents them from being drowned by the outflow of wine.[70]

These quaint characteristics apart, over £100,000,000 is spent annually in the USA on the control of wood-eating termites, over £1 million is spent every year in repairing buildings in Hawaii that have been damaged by termites, and about $A.6 million in Australia. In addition to their attacks on buildings, termites cause damage to man-made fabrics, plastics (including polythene and PVC) and some metal foils.[73] Their economic importance therefore extends to countries (such as Britain) which export to termite-infested zones.

There are very many animals which prey on termites. Some attack termites in their mounds, some feed on foraging termites, and very many make a banquet of flying termites.

The sudden 'death' of numbers of *Macrotermes natalensis* mounds has been observed in the lower Ivory Coast.[11] This was traced to invasions of the nest by predatory ants, *Dorylus dentifrons,* which attack the mounds at night, breaking open holes in the wall. Even a thick-walled queen cell was broken into when left overnight among the ants.

Perhaps the most familiar predators of termite mounds are the ant-eaters of South America and their counterparts in the Ethiopian zoogeographical region, the pangolins and ant-bears, and the spiny ant-eaters of Australasia. These are all equipped with powerful fossorial front legs and typically have long and sticky tongues which will whip up hundreds of termites at a time. Their preference for termites rather than ants vary. Pangolins are primarily eaters of ants, while ant-bears feed exclusively on termites. Chimpanzees, it has recently been discovered, occasionally feed on termites and a point of great interest is that they use twigs as a tool to collect the insects. The twigs are put into holes prepared for emergence of the winged forms and then withdrawn with soldiers clinging to them.[48]

Birds are important predators of termite swarms; according to de Bont,[30] very few African bird species refuse winged termites. and few termites, if any, escape when a swarm emerges near a flock of swallows or swifts. He believes that they are a basic food for the young of many species of bird. The African Pennant-winged Nightjar hunts winged termites in the evenings, sometimes uniting in large bands to do so. They also undergo a migration, crossing the equator twice a year, and this seems to be linked with the seasonal abundance of winged termites, which appear in the north-east Congo from April to August and in the south for the remainder of the year. It is suggested that insect pests would be a greater menace to the economy of Europe were it not for termites! The explanation of this peculiar paradox is that most of the insectivorous birds of Europe are migrants, which overwinter in Africa in regions where termite swarms are common. Their survival in large numbers is ensured by the rich food supply and when they return to Europe they help to control the numbers of insects there.

Man himself is also a predator on termites. Some Brazilian tribes eat the soldiers, which they extract from opened mounds by waving large leaves about inside the nest and withdrawing them with the soldiers hanging on by their jaws. Elsewhere, the winged forms are captured, often in ingenious traps of leaves or twigs put over the mound. Smeathman considered roasted termites to be superior in taste to shrimps, and even weevils: 'something sweeter, but not so fat and cloying as the caterpillar or maggot of the palm tree, snout-beetle . . . the greatest delicacy of the western world'. However, Koenig in 1779 reported that an excess of the insects is damaging to the health and that one may succumb to a surfeit. Nevertheless, termites are not unusually found in African markets as food, and they are also pressed to extract a cooking oil.

Usage has been found even for the mounds. The material of the mounds is often eaten by primitive tribes, presumably for the mineral salts[8]. The material of the mounds is very fine and sets hard after watering. It has been used for making roads, tennis courts, pottery and bricks (450,000 bricks have been made from one mound). Termites are treated as oracles by the Azande tribe in the Sudan. Two pieces of different kinds of wood are put into a mound and issues are decided according to which piece is attacked by the termites.[127] In the Congo it is reported that members of the Bakutu tribe are put into termite mounds when they die, a procedure that is said to be simple and quite sanitary.[69]

After this brief look at the habits of termites and their importance to man and other animals the time has come to examine their society in more detail.

2

ELEMENTS OF THE SOCIETY

Many of the terms used to describe the elements of the termite society—queen, king, worker, soldier, caste, and so on—are taken from those used in describing human society: such comparisons are very tempting. Caste in human society is very difficult to define; but we tend to think of a caste system as embodying tradition and hierarchy to extreme degrees. The Hindu caste system, for example, has developed over the course of more than 2,000 years and it is commonly held that during this period there was a division into castes of priests, warrior rulers, the common man, and artisans, although these exact divisions are not evident at the present day. In social insects the term caste is used in a basically similar way, for classes of individuals that have become specialists and are easily recognisable because of this.

Aristotle recognised the castes of honeybees, and so did Shakespeare in *Henry V*:

> They have here a King and officers of sorts
> Where some, like magistrates, correct at home
> Others, like merchants, venture trade abroad,
> Others, like soldiers, armed in their stings,
> Make brute upon the summer's velvet buds. . . .

Both Aristotle and Shakespeare made the mistake of attributing the 'government' of the hive to a king, and it was not until 1781 that Swammerdamm, a Dutchman, found that the 'king' was female. This mistake could not be made with termites, for in contrast to other social insects their colonies are headed by a king and a queen. The queen in insect societies is usually the sole source of the individuals through the eggs she lays. She might say, with even greater justification than King Louis, *'L'état, c'est moi'.*

Bee and wasp societies tend to be matriarchal with sterile females forming the worker caste, whilst males are such a burden on the society that they may be thrown out to fend for themselves. Termites differ not only because they possess a king, but because their castes are not adult insects but juvenile forms. The juvenility prevents them neither from becoming soldiers nor from becoming sexually mature. The castes which can be readily distinguished in most termite societies are, then, the primary reproductives (king and queen), the replacement reproductives (juveniles that attain sexual maturity in the absence of the king and queen), and the soldiers and the workers, which are permanently juvenile. In general, both soldiers and workers may be of either sex, although sexual dimorphism is found in many species.

The castes can be considered as precise avenues of development although, as we shall see, these are not always cul-de-sacs. There are a series of developmental stages (instars) leading to an individual of a given caste, but the distinction between workers and developmental forms is not always easily made. In the damp- and dry-wood termites it is not possible, because they have a series of larval forms (without wing-pads) leading to several nymphal stages (with wing-pads), all or none of which might be called workers. In *Zootermopsis nevadensis*, the amount of time spent in various activities varies from instar to instar, gradually increasing during the course of development so that termites of the last larval and first nymphal instar do the greater share of the work in the nest.[91] There is apparently a similarity in *Kalotermes flavicollis*, where individuals of the last larval stage are termed *pseudergates*, or pseudo-workers.[53]

In species such as *Reticulitermes*, the increase in activity of the later instars is more precipitous and it is possible to think of the worker caste as equivalent to several instars. In the higher termites (Termitidae) the worker caste comes to be represented by a particular terminal stage of development characterised by a strikingly higher level of activity compared with the preceding stages. One can then speak of this as a 'true' worker caste.[56]

Nasutitermes lujae has workers which go through instars

without changing their size appreciably, but their behaviour
undergoes changes so that the third instar workers are found more
frequently foraging outside the nest.[133] Differences in behaviour
are often noticeable where soldiers of different sizes exist. This is
not normally so in the damp- and dry-wood termites, but it does
apply to *Macrotermes*, for example. *M. natalensis* has large
and small soldiers which have a different developmental history.
The large soldiers appear almost immediately at any breach in
the nest wall, but the small soldiers flee with the rest of the termites
into the depths of the nest. Strangely, in the very closely related
species *M. ivorensis,* the large soldiers appear almost equally
as cowardly as the small soldiers.[128] In *Schedorhinotermes*, a
termite that forages in covered galleries that it constructs over
tree-trunks, the small soldiers accompany the foraging workers
while the large soldiers stay at home. All this could be taken as
evidence that the differences between behaviour of the soldiers
are largely differences in behavioural thresholds. The termite
with the most ranks appears to be *Acanthotermes acanthothorax*,
which has large, medium, and small soldiers, with the latter in
greatest abundance.[129] To these may be added varieties of the large
soldier, but one of these is a freak in the sense that it carries a
parasitic fly larva in its head capsule. Functional differences in
these soldiers have unfortunately not been investigated.

Although the differences between the behaviour of different
termite species may be great, the morphological differences
among workers and among winged forms tend to be very slight.
This no doubt reflects the fact that these are instruments used for
more or less the same tasks throughout the order. Fortunately
for the taxonomist, one finds very many different modifications
of the head and mouthparts of soldiers which are adaptations for
differing modes of aggressive or defensive behaviour. Similarly,
perhaps, knives and forks do not vary greatly throughout the
world, but there are an enormous number of different devices for
killing people.

Strategies of soldiers

Soldiers are strangely lacking altogether in the genera *Speculitermes* and *Anoplotermes,* but in other species there are often
painful reminders of their presence. Escherich,[43] writing in
1908, described how in his first meeting with *Macrotermes
bellicosus* in Abyssinia he put his hand unsuspectingly in a mass

of termites and immediately received a dozen deep cuts in his fingers from which blood came in streams.

The soldiers of *Zootermopsis* differ strikingly from the other castes in their possession of long powerful jaws. They behave more aggressively and are attracted more easily to the source of any disturbance than are the nymphs, but there is no evidence that there is a different repertoire of behaviour patterns involved. Their different reactions can be explained in terms of lower behavioural thresholds to sensory stimuli. For example, if one attacks a nymph with a needle it will probably run away, but if pestered still further it will adopt a threat posture, standing firm with its mandibles held wide open. This threat posture can be elicited immediately from the soldier. Likewise, reactions to chemical stimuli are more easily elicited than in the nymphs.

It should be borne in mind that the soldiers normally operate within galleries. Here, their effectiveness against intruders will be many times greater than in the open, providing, of course, that they are pointing the right way. The soldiers of many dry-wood termites have mandibles that curve upwards slightly; these can be more efficient in narrow galleries since they can be used to dig into an intruder from below. The soldiers of *Cryptotermes* have heads that are adapted for plugging galleries (Fig. 2a), a habit known as phragmosis. The front part of the head is nearly circular in outline.

It is easy to say that soldier mandibles are adaptive, but this means very little unless it is known how they are used by the insects concerned. Observations recently made by Deligne[31] show very neatly how structure and function are interrelated. The soldier mandibles of most dry-wood termites are among the least specialised; in *Kalotermes* (Fig. 2b) they are robust with large lateral teeth. In action, they move fairly slowly and finish by overlapping slightly, left above right, thereby biting into any enemy like a pair of shears.

In many genera, such as *Cubitermes, Basidentitermes,* and *Macrotermes* lateral teeth are lacking and the mandibles are instead long, thin and pointed. The small soldiers of *Macrotermes* can show two different behaviour patterns. Faced with something their own size they attack with rapid and repeated scissor movements of the jaws. Confronted with a larger and more active adversary they sink their mandibles in and do not let go. The soldiers of *Basidentitermes* (Fig. 2c) also show two kinds of

B

aggressive behaviour. When provoked they close their mandibles extremely rapidly, finishing with them slightly crossed. This action may be repeated. If they are strongly excited they will engage their mandibles in the wound they have caused and cross them right over, so enlarging the wound. They often remain locked in this position.

Some termite soldiers have evolved mandibles with elastic properties, and, making use of energy stored elastically and suddenly released, are able to generate mandibular movements of great force. The mechanism is very like that involved in snapping one's fingers. The *Termes baculi* soldier has mandibles like a pair of forceps (Fig. 2*d*) which in the alarm position have the two plane surfaces pressed together near their tips. With increasing tension of the adductor muscles the mandibles bend against each other. When the teeth at the base of the mandibles touch, the mandibles are displaced sufficiently to slide over each other, which happens with great force. Anything to the left or right of the insect, even the well-armoured soldier of another species, suffers a severe wound.

The soldiers of some species have asymmetrical mandibles which discharge with a clicking sound and may send their owners flying through the air as a result of the energy released. This has often been interpreted as a neat method of giving an alarm sound and getting clear simultaneously, but this is probably a mis-interpretation. The behaviour is usually directed at intruders, and Escherich[44] has described how the *Capritermes* soldiers that he observed in Ceylon dealt with invaders of another species.

Fig. 2 (*a*) Head of the phragmotic soldier of *Cryptotermes cavifrons*, (*b*) ventral view of the head of the *Kalotermes flavicollis* soldier in which the extent of movement of the mandibles is indicated by the arrows, (*c*) head of the soldier of *Basidentitermes* with the mandibles in the 'alarm' position—when the aggressive motivation is very high the mandibles, when they are closed together, are crossed to the extent indicated by the dotted arrows, (*d*) sequence of mandibular movements of the *Termes baculi* soldier, 'alarm' position, tension, and discharge positions, (*e*) action of the mandibles of the soldier of *Pericapritermes magnificus*, 'alarm' position and position after release of the catch mechanism, (*f*) soldier of *Armitermes neotenicus*—a form intermediate between jawed soldiers and nasutes.

(*a*) after Banks and Snyder[5], (*b*), (*c*), (*d*), and (*e*) after Deligne[31], and (*f*) after Emerson[40].

The left mandibles of this species are peculiarly curved and when placed under the enemy shoot it forwards and upwards. Confronted with a large invasion, Escherich found that 'a real bombardment resulted, in which one after the other was batted out of the arena in an arc 20–30 cm high.'

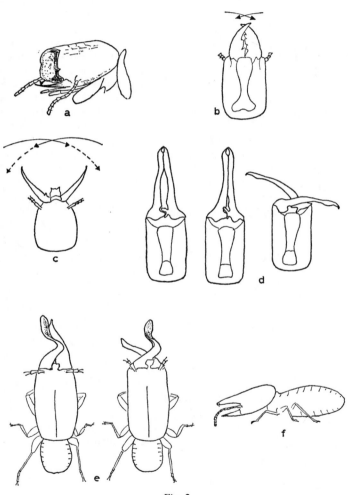

Fig. 2

The technique of the soldier of the African termite *Pericapritermes magnificus* (Fig. 2e) is as follows. The right mandible braces against the left, which is kept more or less rigid. (This, in fact, explains the asymmetry of the mandibles.) The left one is well constructed to act as a brace and when it is bent almost at right angles by the pressure of its partner the latter is released suddenly and with great force. The blow is thus made to the left of the insect, which if necessary will first orientate itself so that the adversary lies to its left. The percussive power developed by this mechanism is considerable and the effect on other insects has been described by Kaiser,[96] who observed the behaviour of the South American species, *Neocapritermes opacus,* in glass tubes with soldiers of other species. The odds turned out to be very unequal: nasute soldiers were frequently decapitated by the blow and the head capsules of the somewhat tougher *Cornitermes* soldiers were shattered.

It is thus possible to see that among termites various kinds of weapons have been developed. Termites have not actually invented gunpowder, although some insects, for example the Bombardier beetle, have come remarkably close to this, but they have gone in for chemical warfare. This is developed very well in the nasute soldiers in which the head is prolonged forward into a nozzle (Fig. 2f). The head capsule contains a reservoir into which numerous glandular cells open. A liquid secretion is shot out from the nozzle and this secretion becomes viscous and sticky in the air. Any adversary can quickly become immobilised from the attacks of a group of these soldiers which will cover him in a sticky web. Ernst[42] made a high-speed film of the behaviour of *Nasutitermes* soldiers in order to analyse their strategy. He found that a 'foreign' insect, in this case a fruit-fly, did not evoke a directed reaction from the soldiers until it was about 1·5 cm away. They then pointed their syringes towards the fly. When the fly came within a distance of 1–2 mm of a soldier it would then usually spray its secretion over the fly (Plate I). The secretion itself acted as an alarm substance for other soldiers; forceps that had been sprayed would sometimes provoke further attacks. In attacking, the soldier thrusts its head towards the enemy and at the same time the contraction of dorso-ventral head muscles causes the emission of the secretion in a fine jet. The termite, of course, has to avoid being caught in its own snare, and it does this by immediately withdrawing and wiping the end of the thread on to the ground. A variant on this behaviour is produced for a slightly more distant fly. The nasute then ejects its spray with a side-to-side movement of its head so that the fly is completely covered.

Moore[125,126] has made an analysis of the secretions of some Australian nasutes. He found that the secretion was mainly various volatile terpenes with a resin composed of several related terpenoids. In air the terpene solvents rapidly evaporate leaving the resinous mixture. It appears that the nasutes are able to synthesise these substances.

The nasutes and the 'jawed soldiers', as the Germans call them, are two fundamentally different types, but nevertheless intermediates exist between them and it is possible to see how the nasutes might have evolved from jawed soldiers. *Armitermes* is an intermediate form with functional biting mandibles and a small syringe. (Fig. 2*f*).

Another kind of intermediate form is found in members of the South American genus *Rhinotermes*. They have an incompletely formed syringe with the nozzle in the form of a groove curved around towards the dorsal surface. The frontal gland, which may extend right back into the abdomen of the insect, opens by a pore into the proximal end of the groove. When the abdominal muscles contract, a defensive fluid is expelled along the groove.

Chemical defence does not seem to be practised by the dry- or damp-wood termites, but it has been found to exist, rather unexpectedly, in *Mastotermes darwiniensis*, although the soldiers of this species have well-developed mandibles. They produce a highly odorous colourless fluid from the mouth which sets into a dark, rubber-like material that has an immobilising effect on other insects. The fluid has been found to contain quinones which are very reactive and set on combining with proteins in the saliva.[125]

Coptotermes lacteus soldiers also produce a rubber-like secretion which has a defensive function. This differs from that of *Mastotermes* in that it is produced from the frontal gland in the head and hardens into a colourless thread simply by drying. It consists of a suspension of lipids and aqueous mucopolysaccharide.

Substances which an animal secretes to the outside of its body and which have an effect on behaviour or on physiological processes in others of the same species are known as pheromones. In ants, pheromones are found in the form of trail substances and alarm substances. Some female moths produce pheromones which are very powerful sexual attractants to the males, and queen honey bees produce a 'queen substance' which inhibits the formation of new queens. It has been found that sex attractants tend to be substances of fairly high molecular weight, which is a reflection of the fact that the molecules must be fairly elaborate for them to be specific. Ant alarm pheromones, in contrast, have been found to have little specificity, i.e. that of one species will excite another, but they are typically very volatile substances that will spread alarm rapidly over a small area. In a study on the ant *Acanthomyops claviger*[134] it emerged that compounds with 10–13 carbon atoms have a vapour pressure high enough to broadcast over a centimetre or so for a period of a few seconds during which the insect remains very sensitive to them.

In view of the relationship between efficiency and molecular weight of pheromones it is interesting that the only true alarm pheromone found so far in termites is limonene ($C_{10}H_{16}$), which has been isolated from *Drepanotermes rubriceps*. Ernst's observation that the defensive secretion of the soldier *Nasutitermes* also acts as an alarm substance is then particularly interesting, since the terpene solvents that have been identified in nasute secretions all have the general formula $C_{10}H_{16}$.

Anoplotermes, it will be recalled, does not possess soldiers, but Grassé and Noirot[57] have been able to see soldier-like behaviour among the workers in a column of termites leaving the nest, which were in constant danger from ants in the vicinity. The column of termites was flanked by an echelon of aggressive workers pointing outwards. Such behaviour is common with the soldiers of species that have foraging trails above ground, such as the nasute species. Ants in the vicinity approached the column with great circumspection. Very strangely, any termites that were killed, usually by attack from the rear, were left lying there by the ants, and were still untouched twenty hours after the procession had passed. This aversion can only be explained in terms of the production by the termites of some volatile substance that is extremely unpleasant to the ants, so effective in fact that weapons in the form of jaws are superfluous. *Trinervitermes* has nasute soldiers which were seen to defend a similar column efficiently against ants, spraying them with 'glue' which had a toxic as well as a disabling effect, but the dead termites, including the soldiers, were taken away by the ants.

3

STRUCTURE AND FORMATION

OF COLONIES

The number of soldiers in a colony of termites depends upon the species and is also affected by the size of the colony and the season. The soldier caste, absent in *Anoplotermes* and *Speculitermes,* composes less than 0.1% of the colony in *Amitermes laurensis,* but in most species about 5% of the individuals are soldiers. The soldier frequency is very variable in small colonies of *Kalotermes flavicollis,* but in colonies of more than 280 individuals it is around 3%.[112] The maintenance of a particular ratio suggests the existence of a mechanism for the replacement of soldiers when their numbers fall and for their elimination when they are present in excess proportions. This brings us to a very challenging problem in biology: just how is this regulation achieved? Before entering into this question it will be useful to emphasise again that a fundamental difference between other social insects and termites is that in the latter the castes are formed from young individuals whose growth is 'frozen' or arrested at certain points. Also, whereas in other insects the castes are often determined genetically (e.g. all honeybee workers are females) the castes of many termite species, though not all, contain equal sex ratios and the evidence is that any individual, at least for some period of its life, is capable of differentiating into any of the castes. The situation is therefore analogous to those often encountered in developmental biology, where particular cells of an embryo can at various stages be induced to develop in different directions according to external influences.

Caste determination

Much of the basis of our present knowledge of caste regulation
in termites was laid by an American, Castle,[24] who investigated
Zootermopsis angusticollis, and Light[103–4] and his colleagues who
studied *Z. nevadensis*. In the latter insect, the population of soldiers
in colonies collected in the field was found to lie between 0·49
and 12·49%, varying throughout the year. Individuals have to
undergo two moults to the soldier form, the first results in an
intermediate called the 'white soldier' which exists for a relatively
short time. Occasionally, colonies are found with high proportions
of white soldiers—so-called 'soldier flares'. These appear to result
when the soldier ratio falls too low.

Plainly, for soldier numbers to be regulated within certain
proportions, there must be some measure of the relative numbers
of soldiers in a colony which can be used to stimulate soldier
production or induce their elimination. It is believed that pheromones are concerned, and there is good evidence for control by
inhibition. Castle found that just one soldier was produced among
the first young of new colonies of *Z. angusticollis*. During the
first year, no further soldiers appeared unless the existing one
was removed. In this event, a replacement was usually produced
after about a month, and in one colony five soldiers were produced as successive replacements. However, a soldier was *not*
produced if a white soldier from another colony was introduced.
In the other species (*Z. nevadensis*) the situation was found to be
similar: the first individual to hatch became a soldier. When a
white soldier was introduced into young colonies there was
inhibition of soldier formation in over 95% of the tests. But
when fully formed soldiers were introduced these either became
very aggressive and were destroyed by the colony or were walled-
off by the other termites and soon died as a result.

There is good evidence, then, not only for inhibition of soldiers
by soldiers, but of sensitivity of colonies to different degrees of
soldierness. This sensitivity could account for both production
and elimination of soldiers. Considered from the point of view
of specialisation into castes, though, *Zootermopsis* stands at a
relatively primitive level. It appears that the pathway to soldier
development in a young colony can be blocked or opened by the
presence or absence of a soldier. This is not necessarily so in other
species. Only 65% of the young colonies of *K. flavicollis* developed

soldiers[60] and only a minority of *Reticulitermes*[162] colonies did so. It must be assumed that the stimulus to soldier production here is something more than a low level of inhibitory pheromone. An interplay of two or more pheromones could actually be an advantage because it would permit closer control over soldier ratios. A further means of enhancing regulation would be through genetic determination, and this has been found to exist, in part, in Termitidae. For example, all the soldiers of *Macrotermes natalensis* are female and all the soldiers in *Trinervitermes* are male.[129]

To return to the more primitive termites, elegant experiments have recently thrown light on the physiological processes of soldier formation. Soldiers have been produced in *K. flavicollis* by the implantation of glands into the sixth instar larvae.[116] In order to understand these experiments it will be useful to know a little about the endocrine system of insects.

A group of nerve cells in the *pars intercerebralis* of the brain (Fig. 3a) produce not nerve impulses, but secretions which they pass directly to glands known as the *corpora cardiaca* and the *corpora allata*. The latter produce a juvenile hormone, and only when their activity is suppressed by the neurosecretory cells of the brain do the characters of the adult insect develop. The moulting cycle is controlled by a hormone released from the prothoracic gland (usually called the ventral gland in termites) and this in turn is activated by brain neurosecretory cells.

Injection of the moulting hormone, ecdyson, into *K. flavicollis* will induce moults but will not, by itself, influence the caste of the individual. However, Lüscher and Springhetti[116] found that they could produce soldiers from sixth instar larvae by implanting into them corpora allata taken from other soldiers, or from reproductives, or from nymphs ready to moult into winged reproductives. The corpora allata of cockroaches are known to produce a hormone which stimulates egg production in adult females. It appears that this 'gonadotropic hormone' is in fact responsible for the formation of soldiers, although recent work has shown it to be identical with juvenile hormone. The different effects are due to different concentrations of the hormone.

Lebrun[101] has recently performed a wide range of transplantation experiments with *K. flavicollis*, in which he confirmed and extended the findings of Lüscher and Springhetti. He found that not only did implantation of corpora allata of replacement reproductives

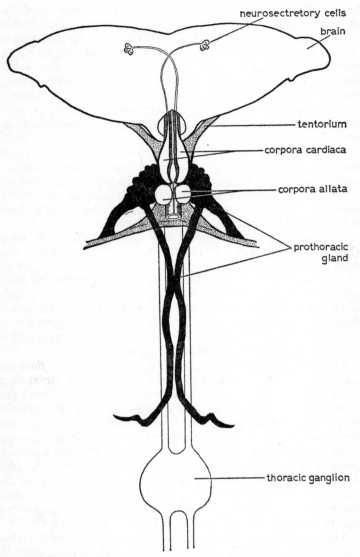

neurosectretory cells

brain

tentorium

corpora cardiaca

corpora allata

prothoracic gland

thoracic ganglion

Fig. 3 The endocrine system of *Kalotermes flavicollis*
(after Lüscher[109, 111]).

give rise to soldiers or soldier-pseudergate intercastes, but that implantation of the corpora allata of sexually mature female cockroaches had the same effect. Lebrun suggests that when the corpora allata hormones are present in large amounts, they block the path to reproductive development, so that development is diverted to the soldier line. A further interesting discovery was that soldiers could be produced with greater certainty if, after implantation of corpora allata, ventral glands were implanted to precipitate an early moult. Lüscher and Springhetti, however, have not been able to produce this effect with ecdyson.

It is possible to conclude, then, that the termites that moult to soldiers are those which have a high concentration of juvenile hormone in their blood, which results from high corpora allata activity. Lebrun believes that a further link in this chain is provided by pheromones from the reproductives which act by stimulating the corpora allata activity. This being so, it could explain why soldiers are quickly produced in young colonies, but it would not mean that soldiers did not give off an inhibitory pheromone as well.

It has been known since 1893[64] that in the absence of the king and queen that founded the colony, replacement reproductives develop. These are larval or nymphal forms which are sexually mature. Such forms are met with sporadically in the animal kingdom (e.g. in Amphibia) and are known by the general term of *neotenics*. Again, evidence has accumulated to show that reproductives have an inhibitory effect on the formation of further reproductives. In *Zootermopsis* the presence of the original pair inhibits the formation of neotonics, but if the colony is orphaned replacements are soon produced. Isolated individuals of *K. flavicollis* tend to develop into replacement reproductives.

The production of neotenics in *K. flavicollis* has been examined in some detail by Lüscher. The various paths of development open to the individuals are shown in Table 1. The sixth larval stage may in reality be a series of stages, because the insects may moult at regular intervals without change in form. Nymphs may also go into reverse and moult back to sixth stage larvae. These individuals are known as *pseudergates,* or false workers. One of four things can happen to a pseudergate when it moults: it can either stay as it is, become a white soldier (presoldier), become a nymph with wing-pads, or become a replacement reproductive.

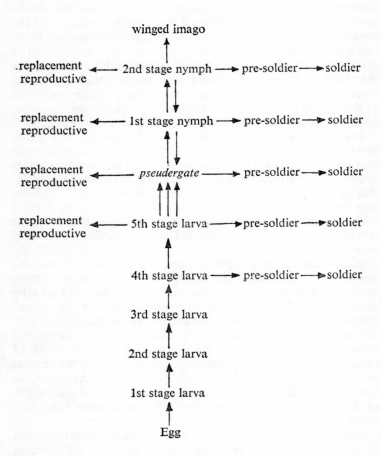

Table 1

The course of development in *Kalotermes flavicollis*. The arrows indicate moults, but several moults lead from the 5th stage larva to the pseudergate. (Modified from Lüscher, 1961)[112]

In *Zootermopsis* replacement reproductives can sometimes be relatively numerous, but in *K. flavicollis,* and perhaps in all dry-wood termites, they are limited to a single couple. This is achieved by the elimination of supernumerary individuals. It has been found that the elimination resulted from fighting among the reproductives.[141] No fighting occurred if their antennae were amputated and the stumps varnished over, but if reproductives with intact antennae were introduced they survived at the expense of the others. The presumption is clear that chemoreceptors on the antennae are involved in releasing the aggressive behaviour.

The aggressive behaviour begins with one particular reproductive picking on one particular subject. The aggressor begins by making rapid antennal movements every time it meets its potential victim. These soon give way to biting movements, to which the other responds by turning to present to the aggressor the inner curve of the abdomen which is relatively difficult to bite. There may be a number of encounters like this until the victim is actually wounded. At this juncture, the aggressor retires from the scene. The larvae, nymphs and soldiers of the colony, apparently attracted by the blood of the insect, then indulge in cannibalism to complete the elimination. While cannibalism is to us a highly unsociable habit, to say the least, the reverse is true of termites. Injured and dead individuals are a potential danger to the colony because they could support disease. Ants, such as the wood ant (*Formica rufa*) and the fire ant (*Solenopsis*), take their dead to a communal rubbish dump away from the nest. Termites take the alternative course of eating their fallen confederates while they are still fresh and juicy.

Although the pseudergates can differentiate in any of the different directions shown in Table 1, their course of development can be changed only if they are within a critical period that follows the moult. The percentage of individuals that are able to develop into replacement reproductives at the next moult declines exponentially with time. By analogy with developing cells these individuals are said to be competent. The competence appears to be related to the activity of the corpora allata, which increase in size after the moult and then decrease again but reach another maximum just before the next moult.[113]

Attempts to isolate a substance responsible for inhibition of neotenics has so far failed in *K. flavicollis,* but it has been possible to show which end of the body it comes from! Lüscher[112] fixed a female reproductive in a solid screen dividing two colonies. Neotenics were produced only in the colony furnished with the head, showing that an inhibitory substance must be given off by the abdomen. This inhibition was maintained if the cuticle of the abdomen was varnished over, but not if the anus was blocked. Therefore it seems that the pheromone arises or is liberated in the gut and passes out with the faeces. The same may possibly prove to be true in *Zootermopsis nevadensis* where Light was more fortunate with his extracts and found that those of the head and thorax and of the viscera of neotenics had inhibitory effects.

Detailed investigations of sexual inhibition have revealed a remarkable complexity.[113] Male neotenics inhibit the formation of further males, and females that of further females in *K. flavicollis*. Females are more readily produced and are more efficient inhibitors than males, but the inhibitory action of a male is enhanced if a second male is present and is complete if a female is present.

The reproductives, therefore, stimulate each other to give off sex-specific inhibitory pheromones. This is not the end of the story, since removal of reproductives from a colony for a period of only twenty-four hours is enough to trigger off the formation of replacements, while the existence of only one reproductive in an even larger colony is sufficient to repress replacements of the same sex. The idea that all the members of a large colony come into contact with the sexual forms in twenty-four hours is scarcely credible. The rapid transmission is achieved by the pseudergates acting as 'middle men'. This was shown by fixing pseudergates in a screen between two colonies, making them a possible transmission channel for pheromones. With a reproductive pair at the head end, inhibition resulted at the tail end. Strangely, male pseudergates tended to inhibit the formation of female neotenics, and *vice versa*. Although the psuedergates act as transmitters they do so in a perverse fashion, apparently taking in the pheromone appropriate to one sex and transmitting that of the opposite sex.

Yet another complexity exists in the form of a *stimulatory* pheromone. Evidence for this has been found only in male reproductives, which give off a substance that stimulates the production of females. The effect can be achieved by an extract of the heads of neotenics and the pheromone is possibly a precursor of the inhibitory pheromone which is produced in the presence of the sexual partner.

Thus, one may say that although none have been isolated, there is excellent *prima facie* evidence for the existence of a number of pheromones which circulate among the members of a colony of *K. flavicollis*. Some of these pheromones inhibit, some stimulate, affecting either the behaviour of individuals or the activity of their endocrine glands. In a 'normal' colony these pheromones achieve steady-state concentrations but if there is a significant disturbance in the caste ratios, the pheromone balance throughout the colony alters rapidly so that changes are initiated to redress the balance. In the production of soldiers, the pheromone imbalance evidently acts by stimulating corpora allata activity and thus causing secretion of juvenile hormone. Lebrun[101] argues that in the production of replacement reproductives the pheromone imbalance stimulates the activity of the ventral glands, which produce the moulting hormone ecdyson. A proportion of the termites will thus be induced to undergo premature moults. Where these are very premature, the insects may still be competent, and will tend to differentiate into replacement reproductives. The large amount of juvenile hormone in their blood may be the factor that causes degeneration of their ventral glands, a feature that accompanies sexual maturity, as in other insects. An alternative explanation, due to the work of Lüscher and his colleagues, is that changes in the ventral gland are secondary to changes initiated elsewhere (for example in the brain) by a pheromone imbalance.

There are, perhaps, two morals to this story. Firstly, that the investigations of a problem that could be very simply conceived has revealed a system of daunting intricacy. Secondly, that the stability of caste ratios in termites must be of paramount importance in termite colonies from an evolutionary point of view, otherwise such a complexity of physiological feedbacks and safety valves would not have arisen.

It must be emphasised that the description so far applies only to *Kalotermes* and *Zootermopsis* and, even then, what applies to the one does not necessarily apply to the other. Mechanisms of caste determination in other termites may be radically different. A certain amount of research that has been done on *Reticulitermes*, for instance, shows that generalisations are best avoided. Neotenics were produced in colonies of *R. hesperus*, when the primary king and queen were still present, by mechanical agitation of the workers.[18] Also, in contrast with the situation in *Zooter-mopsis*, the production of soldiers apparently depends on some environmental feature that is rare in young colonies. Further details of differences of the make-up of the societies of other species would be tedious to enumerate, but an important discovery has been made by Noirot,[129] who found as a result of patient research that genetic mechanisms intervene in the caste determination of many of the 'higher' termites.

The extent to which sex determines caste is a theme with many permutations and combinations. *Nasutitermes arborum* has large workers which are always females and small workers which are always males. Soldiers may develop from either, but normally develop from the male workers.

Table 2 shows the schemes of development for two further examples: *Microcerotermes* and *Macrotermes natalensis*. *Microcerotermes* has two larval stages preceding the workers, whereas *Macrotermes,* in contrast with other genera, has three. In both species, sexual dimorphism is evident after the first moult.

Swarming and colony foundation

Very little is known about the way in which the winged termites develop, but as in other insects the corpora allata must play a part. The winged forms derive from nymphs with long wing-pads, which are usually present in the colony months before the flight, and whose appearance is related to cyclic changes that take place in the activity of the colony. These cycles can usually be related to the seasons. In the Pyrenees *K. flavicollis* swarms in autumn, and then from the beginning of November until the end of April no eggs are laid and the development of the termites is at a standstill. In the summer, nymphs which have been present in the colony since the previous autumn undergo moults to winged forms, and soldiers are also produced in their maximum numbers about this time.[60]

In many tropical regions, where the temperature varies very little throughout the year, the time when the long-winged nymphs are produced (and also the time of swarming) is generally related to the cycle of rains. Thus in the Ivory Coast, nymphs of *Cubitermes fungifaber*[12] appear after the rains and continue to develop during the dry season. They moult to winged forms in April and the flight takes place a month later at the beginning of the rainy season.

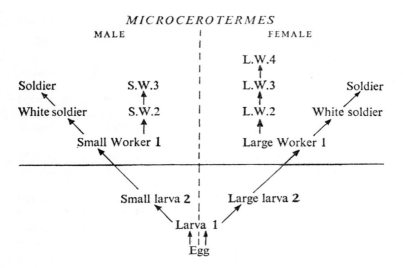

MICROCEROTERMES

MALE | FEMALE

L.W.4

Soldier   S.W.3 | L.W.3   Soldier

White soldier   S.W.2 | L.W.2   White soldier

Small Worker 1 | Large Worker 1

Small larva 2 | Large larva 2

Larva 1

Egg

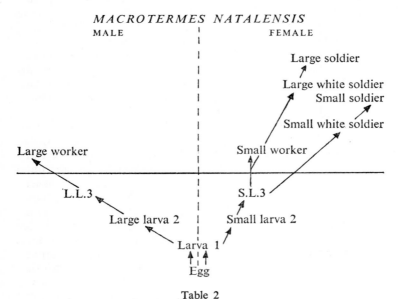

MACROTERMES NATALENSIS

MALE | FEMALE

Large soldier

Large white soldier
Small soldier

Small white soldier

Large worker | Small worker

L.L.3 | S.L.3

Large larva 2 | Small larva 2

Larva 1

Egg

Table 2

Course of development of the castes of *Microcerotermes* and *Macrotermes natalensis*. Male soldiers are formed only exceptionally in *Microcerotermes* (after Noirot, 1955)[129]

Cycles such as this are not present in such a marked form in all species. In the dry-wood termite *Neotermes tectonae*[97] winged forms are present in the nest for most of the year, and the swarming period extends from October until December. In another dry-wood termite, *Cryptotermes havilandi*,[166] the swarming period extends over most of the year at Port Harcourt, but the number of winged termites caught in a trap showed an excellent inverse relationship with the annual cycle of rainfall. In *Macrotermes* and many other mound-building species, on the other hand, a single swarm is usual, with possibly one or a few smaller swarms around the same time.

The timing of swarms can be extraordinarily precise, and not only from the seasonal aspect. Harris and Sands[75] report that two species of *Pseudacanthotermes* living in the same area in Uganda swarm on the same days, but one at two o'clock in the afternoon and the other three and a half hours later. Differences in swarming habits will tend to prevent hybridisation, and it is scarcely surprising to find that there is little uniformity in the swarming habits of different species, suggesting that there are quite a range of environmental cues to emergence that have been exploited by different species. Nevertheless, although the same species may swarm at the same time (and on the same day even at points hundreds of miles apart) differences do exist within species. One example is that of *Macrotermes natalensis* which swarms at around five o'clock in the morning in Uganda and the Congo, but shortly after night-fall in the Ivory Coast.[140]

Preparations for a flight may begin several days beforehand. In *M. natalensis,* workers build special galleries between the ducts inside the mound and outside, where they show as horizontal slit-like openings in the wall. Some species construct special chimneys around the openings of emergence galleries situated around the nest. This is seen in *M. gilvus* in Indochina,[71] where the chimneys are about 5 cm high and 1 cm wide. While these are under construction a 'guard' of small and large soldiers surrounds them. Other species, such as *Coptotermes*, construct ledges around the emergence holes, which are regarded as launching platforms.

Reticulitermes lucifugus kept under laboratory conditions was found to swarm all the year round, but the winged forms were produced mainly in March and April.[77] The most effective cue for emergence was a change in light intensity. When the colonies were kept in a dark room swarming started immediately the light was switched on, and could be stopped simply by switching the light off again. Watering the nest could also provoke swarming, which occurred after a delay of four to eight hours. Swarming was also noted to coincide with the sudden pressure and other climatic changes associated with 'Föhn' weather in southern Europe. It seems, therefore, that in nature a conjunction of climatic factors will control the times of swarming.

Swarming in *M. natalensis* is also timed by climatic factors, but in a complicated way, as a recent investigation in the Congo by Ruelle[140] has shown. Adults taken from the nest before the flight are capable of flying immediately and will indeed do so and found new colonies afterwards. Evidently, they normally stay in the mound until some environmental cue motivates all of them to leave together. Another stimulus must also initiate the preparations for the flight, which are discernible only a few days in advance.

Ruelle found that the flights took place in the early morning between 4.30 and 5.30 am on calm nights when the previous day

Year	Date of Flight	First Rains	Days between flights & 1st rains	Experiment	Date of induced or delayed flight
1959	Oct. 15	Sept. 20	25	—	
1960	Sept. 30	Sept. 20	10	Watering nest	Sept. 17
1961	Oct. 5	Sept. 20	15	Nest covered by tent	Oct. 15 Nov. 18
1962	Oct. 13	Sept. 28	15	—	
1963	Oct. 12–13	Sept. 24	18	One nest watered One nest covered by tent	Sept. 26, 27 & 28 Dec. 7

Table 3

The timing of emergence of swarms in nests of *Macrotermes natalensis* near Kinshasa (after Ruelle, 1964)[140]

had been very warm. They occurred ten to twenty-five days after the onset of the rainy season. (The details for five years are summarised in Table 3.) Ruelle experimented to see if he could alter the emergence times in some of the nests. In 1961 he soaked a nest with 425 litres of water over a period of fifteen days, with the result that the flight occurred much earlier than in other mounds. A similar outcome resulted from repeating the experiment in 1963. Covering a nest completely with a plastic tent in 1961 retarded the flight but also slowed the process of development of the winged forms from the nymphs. However, retarding of the flight was achieved when a nest was partially covered with a tent, so that the rain was kept off but a free circulation of air was possible. None of these measures was sufficient to *prevent* emergence which occurred eventually as a 'vacuum activity' indicating that social factors can have a role in starting the swarm.

On the basis of his findings, Ruelle concluded that the direct action of rain on the mound was the factor that released the preparations for flight. The rain, of course, could have various effects on the mound: a purely mechanical effect, a wetting of the wall, a lowering of temperature, a change in humidity in the galleries, and an interference in gas exchange across the wall. The temperature and the carbon dioxide and humidity levels in the nest all vary in a cyclic fashion throughout the day, and it seems unlikely that they provide the major cue to emergence. Neither pouring water into the mounds, injecting carbon dioxide, nor inducing temperature changes by sheltering the nest or putting blocks of ice around it had any effect on emergence. Ruelle considers the most likely cue to be the mechanical effect of raindrops on the hive, and he supports this by quoting observations that the Africans in some regions beat tom-toms or hit the surface of the mound with branches in order to provoke swarms. The matter is still not completely resolved, but it appears likely that in their practices of pouring water on mounds and beating them the Africans have long anticipated scientific discovery.

The synchronised flights of many species sometimes result in the skies being clouded with the insects so that mixing of swarms from different colonies is highly likely. Pairing commonly begins when the insects have finished their flight, but there are exceptions. *Pseudacanthotermes* males, for instance, seize the female in flight with their mandibles, shed their wings in the process, and finish the flight as passengers.[75]

Allodontotermes giffardii flies in the Ivory Coast in broad daylight several hours after rain.[13] A peculiarity of this species is that the females do not fly after emergence, but climb on to grass stems and adopt a 'calling posture' with the abdomen pointing upwards (Plate I). Intermittent fanning movements are made with the wings, propelling the air upwards over what is probably an exposed scent gland. The males are poor fliers and travel less than 15 m away from the nest, but they then assemble in the area where the females are displaying. The male assumes a position behind the calling female, grasping her—as it were—with his antennae. The pair then move off in tandem, maintaining this relative position. Among the leaf litter they lose their wings and subsequently (if they survive the attentions of predators) dig a chamber for themselves in which a new colony begins.

This species apart, it is usual for both sexes to take part in the flight. Insects that have flown lose both their wings on settling. Tropical species appear to shrug their shoulders and the wings drop off, in an action that is too swift to follow, breaking at a line of weakness near the base. As it is impossible to achieve the fracture by pulling the wings with a pair of forceps, it must be that the plane of movement is important. *Zootermopsis* adults can be induced to shed their wings *before* they have flown by lowering a glass plate on to them from above until it just touches them. This releases a curious waltzing movement, in which they turn first to one side and then to the other. This results in the wing-tips getting caught from time to time and they tend to be rotated forwards on their axes. Multiple cracks gradually develop in the wings near the fraction plane and the wings break off one by one. In the higher termites, such as *Cubitermes,* rotation is less effective, and a downward bending strain appears to be important.[167]

The tandem usually begins after the wings have been shed. In *Kalotermes* or *Zootermopsis*, where the shedding of wings is a relatively clumsy process, the interattraction of the male and female is not very strong; the pair sometimes lose each other and sometimes males will follow males and females follow females. The tandem may last up to two days. In the *Termitidae*, in contrast, the procedure follows with much greater precision. *Microtermes aluco* males grasp the abdomen of the female with their mandibles.[127] Several males will compete in this ungentlemanly fashion for one female. If they are detached they fight each other, attacking the mandibles, which suggests that their 'courtship' behaviour (if one may call it that) is directed by a pheromone produced by the abdomen of the female. A more usual occurrence in the higher termites is for the female to adopt the calling posture after settling, with her abdomen in the air. In this, the terminal abdominal segments are parted slightly, suggesting the exposure of a scent gland, and the males then run more or less directly towards the female. Unfortunately, no detailed studies have yet been made of this presumed scent gland.

There are a few further points of contrast with the 'lower' termites. Only the females are attractive to the males, and not vice versa, so that the tandem is always male following female. The interattraction is very high, so that the pair do not disengage. In an *Anoplotermes* species observed by Lüscher,[107] the male clambered on to the abdomen of the female and was carried around by her. Also, the tandem lasts for a far shorter time on average; only two to ten minutes in *Pseudacanthotermes spiniger,* for example. One reason for this appears to be the speed of reversal of the reaction to light and gravity, which takes place after the insects have shed their wings.

The tandem behaviour ends with the pair excavating a 'bridal chamber' together. When they have done this, mating occurs and the first brood is reared. An interesting description of the formation of this first chamber in the dry-wood termite, *Cryptotermes havilandi*, is given by Wilkinson.[166]

In Port Harcourt, this species swarms in the dry months of the year about half an hour after sunset. After flying, the winged forms seek out cracks and crevices and can begin the process of founding a new colony only if they find a hole with a diameter of 1·5 to 3 mm. This was shown experimentally by Wilkinson, who presented the animals with a series of holes drilled in wood and found that holes near the lower end of the series were rejected because the insect could not turn around after entering. Holes larger than 3 mm in diameter were difficult for the termites to seal. The sealing of the hole, which is an essential step, involves a very curious behaviour pattern. The termite, having entered, 'inspects' the edges of the hole with its antennae and then with the tip of its abdomen. It then exudes from the anus droplets of a brown solution which are deposited around the circumference of the hole with a vibration of the abdomen that may help in detaching the droplets. This is continued until the hole is occluded by a kind of lattice work of these droplets. The behaviour then changes. The open parts of the lattice are filled with a solution that has a deeper brown colour, and the abdomen is then used as a mallet to thump the droplets of this solution into place. This is done with a series of blows that may continue for up to thirty seconds and bend the lattice outwards with their force. Crystalline elements are visible in the completed plug, indicating that the anal secretion is a special glandular one. A solitary termite builds in a rather half-hearted fashion, but if it is joined by a potential mate it speeds up its activity greatly.

The sequence of events in the pairing behaviour of termites often appears to be a very rigid one, a chain sequence in which the omission of one link means that the rest of the actions cannot take place. This is not usually so in the more primitive termites. *Reticulitermes lucifugus* and *K. flavicollis* can shed their wings without having first flown, and are then capable of tandem behaviour and the formation of new colonies. Males will form tandems with winged females, and male *Reticulitermes* that have lost their wings will even form tandems with workers. Therefore exposure of the scent gland is not an essential link to further actions in these insects. Unpaired females will also bore into wood, so neither is the tandem essential.[145]

In the higher termites, there is evidence that the links are more strongly forged. In several tropical species studied by Lüscher[107] a flight of at least three minutes was necessary before the wings could be shed. Winged forms taken from the nest usually flew spontaneously when brought into the open air, but if the flight was forced by throwing them into the air a number of times, this proved to be adequate for wing-shedding afterwards. Sands[144] also reports that in several species of *Trinervitermes* colony foundation is not possible unless the winged forms have previously taken part in a flight. If they were made to fly by placing them in a strong breeze and were then artificially de-winged, they would enter an artificial nest, but the first cell was not constructed properly and no eggs were laid. Furthermore, when removed from their nest they attempted to fly with their wing stumps. Further evidence for essential links comes from Goetsch,[46] who observed that *Anoplotermes* would not pair after only a short flight. The adults would eventually lose their wings if they did not fly, but they would not then found new colonies.

These observations show that there has been an evolutionary trend towards a closer knitting together of the sequence elements:

a change from 'plasticity' to 'stereotypy'. The advantages to the
termites are obvious, but many biologists consider 'plasticity'
and 'adaptability' to be traits of the behaviour of more highly-
evolved animals, since they imply an ability to modify behaviour
in accord with experience or environmental changes. Perhaps these
terms are rather subjective when applied to behaviour; a point
we shall consider in the last chapter.

The foundation of new colonies without swarming has been
observed by Grassé and Noirot[57] in a species of *Anoplotermes*
and in *Trinervitermes bettonianus*. They saw columns of these
termites emerging in broad daylight and eventually splitting
up into separate groups, each of which built a new nest: a process
the French biologists called *sociotomy*. Sands[143] claims that this
kind of peripatetic swarm is caused by invasions of aggressive
doryline ants into the mound. He observed a colony of *T. oeconomus* leaving its mound, which proved on inspection to be full of
ants. The colony stayed under a tree and returned when the ants
had moved on.

Whatever the cause of the emergence—and Grassé and Noirot
present a number of reasons for believing that ants were not
responsible for what they described—the behaviour is immensely
interesting and almost certainly highly adaptive.

Grassé and Noirot saw a portion of the colony containing all
castes, including the king and queen emerge, and in *Anoplotermes*
termitophiles were also present. In *T. bettonianus* winged forms
were in the column in some numbers, and the workers carried
eggs, larvae, and injured and dead termites; one large worker
was found to be carrying a small one that had lost a foot and
could not walk quickly. The soldiers were found at the rear of
the column and along its sides forming a flank guard 2 to 20 cm
away from the edge.

The presence of winged forms in the convoy is very odd, since
normally they do not leave the nest unless to take part in the

---

Plate I

(a) Nasute soldiers of *Nasutitermes arborum* attacking a fruit-fly.
(Reproduced by permission of E. Ernst.)

(b) Soldiers of *Zootermopsis angusticollis* attacking a praying
mantis by the leg.

(c) Winged adult female of *Allodontotermes giffardii* in the
'calling posture'. (Reproduced by permission of P. Bodot.)

PLATE I

(a)

(b)

(c)

PLATE II

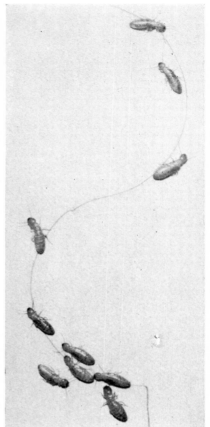

(a)

(b)

(c)

flight. It was observed that their behaviour was very similar to that of the workers; they carried larvae and eggs between their mandibles. In the column they showed no courtship behaviour, but it sometimes happened that some of them lost contact with the stream, and their behaviour then underwent a radical change. They formed tandems and shed their wings, although the females rarely took up anything like the calling posture. After courtship, the termites did not re-enter the column.

The main interest of this behaviour is the way in which normal reactions to stimuli such as light, moving air, and so on, are inhibited or, to look at it from another viewpoint, the way in which the behaviour of all the individuals is unified. A similar phenomenon has been seen by Grassé,[50] who found that workers of *Macrotermes* would carry on their normal building activity around the queen when she was taken from the nest and put in the open air. It is possible to explain this in terms of *'l'effet de groupe'*—a large social group inhibiting aspects of the behaviour of individuals, but it is likely to be understood ultimately in terms of pheromones. Possibly what *Anoplotermes* and *Trinervitermes* have 'discovered' in the course of their evolution is a highly effective trail pheromone that is produced in times of stress and is linked with a following reaction that has a strong inhibitory effect on other behaviour patterns. It will be surprising if continuing research does not show that pheromones play a large part in swarming as well. Synchronous flight in winged forms of a colony of camponotine ants is known to be triggered by the release of a pheromone[83], and this possibility might repay study in termites.

Sense organs and orientation of winged forms

A central feature of the behaviour of flight and colony foundation is the simple but precise changes that occur in the orientation

---

Plate II

(a) Three successive frames from cine film taken at 64 frames/sec, showing the action of the tapping movement of *Zootermopsis angusticollis*.

(b) Termites (*Zootermopsis nevadensis*) following a trail (over the pencil line) of an ether extract of the sternal gland.

(c) Dry-wood termites (*Kalotermes minor*). Soldier (S), replacement reproductive (R), nymph with short wing-pads (N), and larva (L). About 5 × natural size.

of the insects. Winged forms taken prematurely from the nest tend to be positively geotactic (they go downwards), negatively phototactic (they go away from light), and positively thigmotactic (they tend to press together or go into crevices). At the time of swarming these responses are reversed, so that the termites lose contact with each other and their surrounding structures, climb and fly upwards and are attracted to light. Loss of wings after settling appears to cause another reversal of the behaviour so that the insects go downwards, into crevices, and away from light.

These changes have been studied experimentally in *Kalotermes flavicollis* by Richard[135] who found that light and sloping surfaces were two stimuli that could elicit flight. He puts adults on to a surface sloping at 60° to the horizontal and illuminated by a beam of light from one side (Fig. 4). With this apparatus he was able to show which were the sense organs that were concerned in the light and gravity reactions. Under the influence of light and gravity, insects tended to take paths which were resultants between the two (i), for example. With their eyes varnished over, the insect tended to walk up the slope (ii). When the antennae were amputated down to the third segment, then paths were more or less directly orientated up the light beam (iii).

The second segment of the antenna contains a number of regularly-distributed sensilla (chordotonal sensilla) each of which

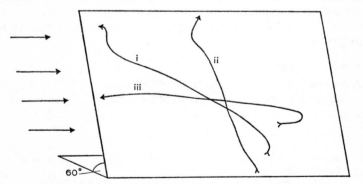

Fig. 4   Typical paths taken by winged *Kalotermes flavicollis* on a sloping surface illuminated by a light beam from the side. (i) normal insects, (ii) blinded insects, (iii) insects with antennae amputated at the third segment (after Richard[135]).

has a peg-like inclusion but no external processes (Fig. 5). Together, these form a complex known as Johnston's organ. This is extremely well developed in mosquitoes where it serves as a hearing organ, responding to vibrations induced in the antenna. It is well situated to do this, because the endings are inserted at the junction between the second segment and the terminal segments which are more of less fused into a single

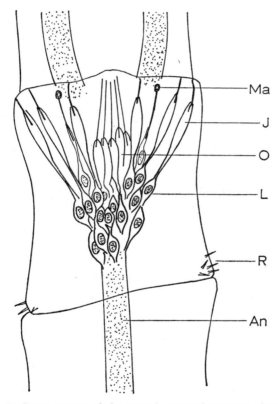

Fig. 5 Sense organs of the second antennal segment of *Zootermopsis angusticollis*. An, antennal nerve; R, group of hair sensilla responsive to movements at the joint; J, Johnston's organ sensillum; L, nucleus of Johnston's organ sensillum; O, sensilla of dorsal chordotonal organ; Ma, campaniform sensilla (responsive to stresses in the cuticle) (from Howse[92]).

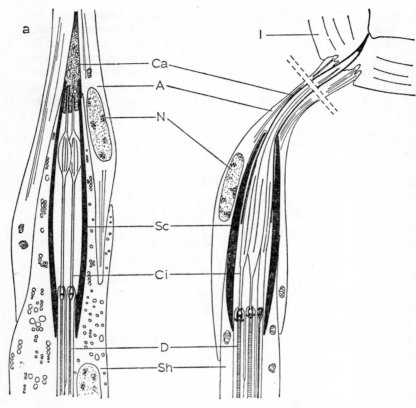

Fig. 6 (a) *above:* Sensilla from the dorsal chordotonal organ of the antenna (left) and from the Johnston's organ (right) of *Zooter-mopsis nevadensis.* I, intersegmental membrane; Ca, cap; A, attachment cell; N, nucleus of attachment cell; Sc, scolopale; Ci, cilium; D, dendrite; Sh, sheath cell of scolopales.

(b) *right:* The subgenual organ of *Zootermopsis angusticollis.* N, main leg nerve; W, V, sensory nerve cell bodies; M, muscle of leg; T, trachea; A, attachment cell; S, scolopales; G, groove in leg wall; P, nerve to campaniform sensilla. The fine structure of the sub-genual organ sensillum is similar to that of the antennal sensilla, except that the cap is more rounded and only one dendrite is present.

(a) reproduced from Howse[92] and (b) from Howse[89].

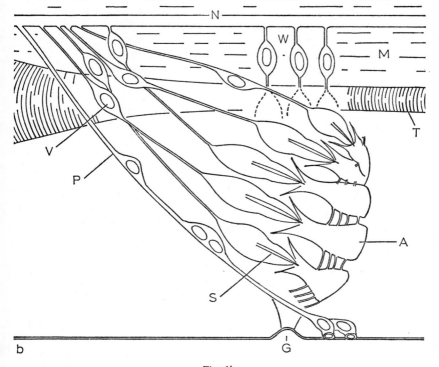

b

Fig. 6b

unit, the flagellum. Richard implicated this organ in the geotactic response in two ways. Firstly, he showed that amputation of the flagellum severely interfered with the gravity response, suggesting that the organ functions by registering the weight of the flagellum. Secondly, he showed that the precision of the gravity response (although it may change direction) improves in individuals as they pass from young larvae to adults, and that this improvement is paralleled by an increase in the number of chordotonal sensilla that comprise the organ, from sixteen in the first stage larva to forty in the adult.[135,137]

The second antennal segment in both *Kalotermes* and *Zooter-mopsis* contains two groups of chordotonal sensilla. One is

Johnston's organ with regularly distributed terminals, and the other is a bunch of sensilla in the upper part of the segment. Experiments on Z. *angusticollis* suggest that while the Johnston's organ may respond to movements of the antenna, the dorsal group is more likely to be the one sensitive to gravity.[89] Examinations of these under the electron microscope have shown that the sensilla differ in structure.[92]

Reconstructions of the two kinds of sensillum, based on electron micrographs, are shown in Fig. 6a. Both consist essentially of a tube formed by fibrous rods (scolopales). Into the base of this tube are inserted two, or three fine nerve terminals. From the tip of each terminal a cilium arises. Each cilium increases markedly in diameter towards its tip, and ends in an extracellular cap. A variety of evidence points to the conclusion that stretch of the membrane of the cilium excites the sense organ. In the sensilla of the dorsal group, this might be achieved by a pull on the cap, which is continued as a long drawn-out thread to attach on to the dorsal wall of the segment. Thus any strains set up in the segment, by the weight of the flagellum for example, might stimulate this receptor.

The cap in the Johnston's organ sensillum is quite different, taking the form of a tube that penetrates right into the joint between the second segment and the flagellum. Thus any movements between the two will compress some of the endings and stretch the membranes of the cilia.

Yet another form of this versatile sensillum plays an important role in the sensitivity of termites to vibration, a phenomenon that will be discussed in the next chapter. This sensillum is found in the subgenual organ, a group of vibration-sensitive cells situated below the knee, which have their caps embedded in cells that are attached to the cuticle (Fig. 6b) and it appears that they respond only to stimuli that cause a flexion in the region of the cap.[92] This means that they are stimulated only by sudden vibrational stimuli, such as taps to the substrate, and that, like insect hearing organs generally, they do not respond to continuous sounds or vibrations unless these contain abrupt intensity changes. The effects of this limitation can be traced to many aspects of insect behaviour. The chirps of crickets and grasshoppers, for example, are very much like a very fast series of clicks. And the vibrations to which termites respond are percussive in character, as are the sounds they produce.

4

COMMUNICATION

It has been known for many years that termites produce tapping noises by means of which they appear to communicate with one another. In fact, according to one authority,[164] Linnaeus originally gave the name *Termes* to the Deathwatch beetle and a true termite. Both produce tapping noises in wood and the tapping of the Deathwatch is often held in folklore to signify the approach of death within the household. Hence the name *Termes,* from the Greek word τέρμα meaning 'the end'.

There are many interesting records in the literature of the sounds produced by termites. One of the earliest is found in the paper that Smeathman delivered to the Royal Society in 1781. He described the 'signal of alarm' made by *Macrotermes* soldiers: 'some of them beat repeatedly with their forceps upon the building, and make a small vibrating noise, something shriller and quicker than the ticking of a watch. I could distinguish this noise at three or four feet distance, and it continued for a minute at a time with short intervals.' Smeathman recorded that, during the process of repairing the nest, an occasional signal from a soldier was immediately answered by a 'loud hiss, which appears to come from all the labourers . . . that it does come from the labourers is very evident, for you will see them hasten at every signal, redouble their haste, and work as fast again'. If there was a further disturbance the workers immediately disappeared into the galleries, and the signal of the soldiers was answered at every stroke with a loud hiss.

The description given above was, of course, of a mound nest

that had been opened, but many species such as *Hodotermes* and *Odontotermes* collect vegetable material from the forest floor. They often make galleries on the underside of dead leaves, cementing them together to form a platform. This is a good sounding-board for taps, and the noise produced by the termites has often been taken for the hiss of a snake. The biologist König, writing in 1779, describes how, on an excursion in India, he was alarmed by a sudden noise and found he had disturbed a column of termites marching through dead leaves. The tapping noise was produced by a jerking movement of the soldiers, and König accordingly named this species *Hodotermes convulsionarius*.[100] A correspondent described to me how he heard a rhythmic clicking sound one night on a cocoa farm in Nigeria. This turned out to be termites tapping synchronously on layers of dead leaves; the sound started when a torch was switched on and stopped when it was switched off. Buxton[23] made a simliar observation of synchronised tapping in the soldiers of *Pseudacanthotermes militaris*. The sound was produced 'in perfect time at a rate of about forty-eight beats per minute, and in the intervals between there was complete silence'.

Significance of sounds

Most people who heard the sound produced by termites assumed it to be an alarm signal. A Swiss scientist, Bugnion,[19, 20] suggested that they could detect the vibrations produced by the tapping, since soldiers on the underside of a sheet of paper were stimulated to tap when the paper was tapped. Some workers believed a more sophisticated system of communication to be present. The Italians Grassi and Sandias[64] studied the convulsive movements of the European termites *Kalotermes flavicollis* and *Reticulitermes flavipes,* and described one convulsive movement which produced no sound and was often repeated at almost the frequency of the pulse rate. This they believed to be a cry to summon help or give alarm, or a lament. It was also reported that the *Reticulitermes* soldier could make a click by rubbing the back of its head against the prothorax. Because they could hear the noise by putting their ears close to wood containing the termites, the Italians suggested that the sound was a form of everyday speech, since it appeared to be a feature of undisturbed nests. Escherich,[43] writing on the convulsive movements of soldiers which did not give rise to tapping noises, considered them to be a means of reminding lazy workers of their duties and inspiring them to greater diligence. Another suggestion has been that sounds of ultrasonic frequency were produced which were conducted through the nest where air pockets acted as resonators.

It is easy to suggest, as most writers did, that the sounds termites produce are involved in a means of communication, but with very few exceptions they did not attempt to find out whether termites could hear. Professor Emerson,[35] however, subjected a nest of *Nasutitermes* to a variety of sounds, using a trumpet and saucepans to generate them, but failed to get the termites to answer back with their tapping. A light tap on the outside of the nest, however, provoked a ready response.

At the present time, the system of communication has been investigated in detail only in the Californian termite *Zootermopsis angusticollis*.[85,86,87] Using a sensitive microphone and modern recording techniques it was found that a pattern of sounds with two clearly recognisable components could be recorded from wood containing these insects (Fig. 7a). There are groups of sounds of relatively high intensity and groups of sounds of relatively low intensity. The obvious inference is that the soldiers produce the former and the larvae and nymphs the latter. This was quite simply shown to be so by separating the castes and putting them into shallow plastic boxes with lids. The larvae

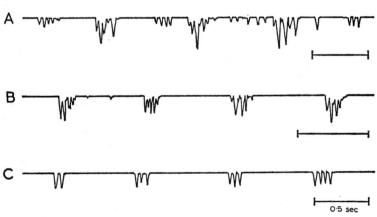

Fig. 7 The pattern of sounds recorded from a colony of *Zootermopsis angusticollis* (A), from soldiers alone (B) and from nymphs alone (C).

were found to produce taps, one to eight at a time (but usually two to three) with fairly regular intervals of about half a second between each spasm of tapping. The individual taps within a group were only about one thirtieth of a second apart (Fig. 7*b* and *c*). The pattern of sounds produced by the soldiers was similar except that there were about twice as many sounds in each group.

When the lids were removed from the top of the boxes, tapping noises could be recorded only from the soldiers. Quite evidently the other forms tap their heads only on the roofs of the galleries while the soldiers also hit the floor on the downstroke. This is clearly shown when the individual frames from ciné film are examined, and the film also shows the way in which the movement is brought about (Plate II). Without changing its position on the ground the termite jerks the forepart of its body up and down by extending and contracting its forelegs. This takes place with extraordinary rapidity: the taps produced may be less than one-thirtieth of a second apart, and in some of the film the termite is caught with its forelegs so rapidly contracted that they have left the ground.

In the dry-wood termites the tapping is not nearly so vigorous, and is more in the nature of a rocking movement. Dry wood is a relatively good conductor of vibration, and therefore perhaps they do not need to expend so much energy in transmitting the signal over comparable distances. The much smaller *Reticuli-termes* have two kinds of very vigorous tapping movements. The first is very similar to that of *Zootermopsis*, repeated at a rate of about 3–4 times per second. If a soldier is excited still further it flattens itself against the ground and then whips up and down by extension and contraction of its forelegs, producing a clearly audible click when the under-surface of the head hits the ground. This may be repeated several times at gradually increasing intervals. This movement is impossible to follow with the naked eye and, again, can only be properly interpreted by examining a record of it on ciné film. The insect is so small and moves so fast that it does not appear to move at all. With this in mind, the report of stridulation in *Reticulitermes* by Grassi and Sandias may possibly be accounted for.

Termites can be stimulated to begin their tapping under a variety of circumstances. When a sensitive microphone was put in with a colony of *Zootermopsis*, tapping was recorded when the nest was exposed to light or when a puff of air was blown in to the container. Sounds of various intensities and frequencies up to 20,000 cycles/sec., emitted from a small loudspeaker suspended above the colony, had no noticeable effect on the termites. But when the loudspeaker was rested against the wood, tapping was recorded in response to stimulation with frequencies between 100 and 1,500 cycles/sec. This confirms that vibrations transmitted through the nest material are detected by the termites, and shows that airborne sound is not detected.

Once the tapping has started in one part of the colony it soon spreads, and as a result of two things: firstly, the excited movement of the termites that are tapping excites others that come into contact with them, and secondly, the detection of vibration itself helps to stimulate tapping in others. An illustration of this was found when the floor under the insects was covered with neoprene, a form of synthetic rubber that transmits vibration poorly. The great majority of tapping movements then occurred when termites came into contact with one another. The reverse was the case without the neoprene.

It has been confirmed that termites detect the tapping noises through the subgenual organs in their legs. By inserting fine electrodes into the leg near to the nerve the electrical signals from the subgenual organ can be picked up, amplified, and recorded. When this was done it was found that the organs are ideally adapted for picking up the tapping noises. They respond best to pulses of vibration delivered at the same rate as the taps, that is several taps or pulses at a rate of about 30/sec., with half-second intervals between each group of vibrations (Fig. 7c). If the pulses are delivered at a faster rate than this, the organ ceases to respond or connections in the nerve from the organ get 'jammed'—it is not yet certain which. The individual taps also have a certain frequency, or pitch—this, of course, is the same as the frequency of the sound we hear when the wood is tapped. This has been analysed and found to be actually a band of frequencies extending over a surprisingly wide range, from about 0 to over 8,000 cycles/sec. in some cases, with a component of greatest intensity around 1,000 cycles/sec. for damp wood, higher for dry wood (Fig. 8a). (The note C, two octaves above middle C on the musical scale, has a frequency of 1,024 cycles/sec.) We naturally hear this mixture of frequencies as a rather dull note, and it was surprising to find that such high frequencies were present. Now, the sensitivity of the subgenual organ at first increases with an increase in frequency, and its point of maximum sensitivity has been measured and found to be at about 1,150 cycles/sec. This remarkable organ is therefore, it appears, tuned to a particular frequency and pattern of sound: that used by the termite. Like a radio receiver that is tuned to a narrow band, the organ is relatively immune to 'interference' in the form of noises of different frequencies and taps of different repetition rates, such as other species of termite might produce.

The temporal patterning of the tapping, which Fig. 8a illustrates to some extent, is very interesting in itself, and leads one

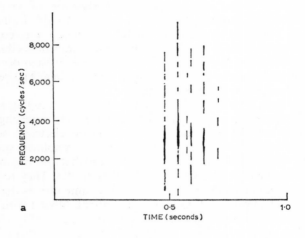

Fig. 8 (a) Sound spectrogram of the taps of a *Zootermopsis angusticollis* soldier showing the wide frequency range of the sounds produced.

(b) Spikes recorded in the nerve from the subgenual organ of *Z. angusticollis* (bottom trace) in response to a pulse of vibration applied to the leg (top trace) later broken up to give 10 pulses/second.

to suspect that the termites might be signalling to each other by some sort of morse code. But when the tapping is analysed there appears to be no evidence at all for any sort of coding. If there was, we would expect to find a pattern of tapping that was variable, different patterns occurring under different circumstances or at different times. Unfortunately perhaps, for it would be exciting to discover something like this, the pattern of tapping is conspicuously inflexible, although some features of it vary with the temperature. For instance there is a change with temperature in the number of taps so that there are relatively more groups of four taps at lower temperatures and relatively more groups of two at higher temperatures, and the intervals between the taps also vary with temperature. This variation is almost certainly without significance, since the activity of cold-blooded animals generally speeds up as the temperature rises. Ants and termites run faster, for example, and it is possible to estimate the temperature from the chirping of some crickets, which gets faster and therefore higher in pitch as the temperature rises.

It is nevertheless clear that termites have a system of communication but in order to see what is communicated one should see if the behaviour of the insects changes when they are subjected to vibration of the substratum. When this was investigated it was found that the termites showed a much greater tendency than usual to go downwards, away from light, and into crevices. They also showed a greater tendency to associate together with their nest-mates or where other termites had recently been present. It therefore seems evident that the vibration produced by the tapping can act as an alarm signal, since it will take the termites away from a breach in the nest wall. At the same time they will tend to aggregate together and follow one another. This would normally mean that they would go in large numbers into the deeper and more inaccessible parts of the nest. A simple experiment illustrates rather graphically the responses that can occur (Fig. 9a). When termites were confined to the centre of a wooden platform inclined at about 30° to the horizontal for several hours, they subsequently showed very little tendency to depart from that area when given the opportunity. (They appear to mark areas they inhabit with pheromones produced from special glands, so that these areas are soon recognised as familiar territory.) The platform was then tapped for a few minutes with a pencil, and the termites all went down to the bottom of

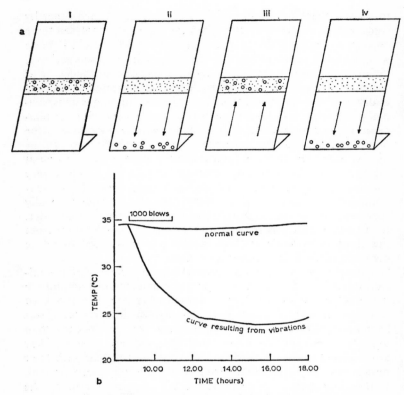

Fig. 9 (a) Diagram of the movements of termites (Z. angusticollis) on a sloping platform when this is tapped.

(b) Graph to show the fall in temperature of the nursery area of a nest of *Coptotermes acinaciformis* after hammering the tree in which the nest was built. The temperature falls because termites leave the nursery area (after Greaves[65]).

the platform (ii), but when the tapping was stopped they gradually began to go upwards again and grouped together in the region from which they had departed (iii). However, when the experiment was repeated and the tapping continued for six to seven minutes the termites then stayed at the bottom of the platform and showed no tendency to return to their original positions (iv).

This gives a picture of what mechanisms might operate in a termite nest, and, happily, observations have been made in the field that suggest something of this nature occurs. Greaves[68] in Australia investigated the distribution of colonies of *Coptotermes* that live in the trunks of living trees. To do this he inserted thermocouples into the trunk at various levels. The temperature was higher where greater numbers of termites were to be found; in the nursery area, for example, the temperature was about 10°C higher than the outside temperature. Greaves gave the trunk of the tree a series of blows with a 10 lb hammer at fifteen minute intervals and recorded the temperature between his exertions. This may sound rather drastic treatment for the termites, but was probably not, as the termite subgenual organ is built to respond to sudden changes and gauges their intensity to only a very limited extent. In this experiment the nursery temperature gradually declined for 3–4 hours (Fig. 9b) indicating that the insects had left the nursery area. They had apparently gone into galleries in the soil around the base of the tree, and did not begin to return and thereby elevate the nursery temperature until about seven hours after the blows had ceased. In *Hodotermes* that collect the seeds of grasses, it has been seen that the soldiers tap on the stem when disturbed, and in response to this the other termites run down the stems and back along their trail to the nest. It may be that in some trails of foraging termites any sudden disturbances in the environment are perceived by the soldiers which typically position themselves at the edge of the trail, and that in response they start their head-tapping which in turn tends to keep the workers on the trail.

Pheromones in communication

There are various sorts of jerking movement shown by termites, which appear to serve different functions. One of these is a particularly vigorous shaking movement; the termite jerks up and down and to and fro in the same complicated movement, which occurs especially when termites have been suddenly disturbed. Following this, the termite runs along rapidly with its abdomen pressed closely to the ground. It appears, again from experiments conducted in the laboratory, that the insect is laying a trail of a chemical substance here, and that the shaking movement is a means of nudging other termites into action. When other termites are excited in this way they will then tend to follow the trail. The evidence points to the fact, however, that there is no intentional communication of information, but that other termites are aroused and then quickly detect and follow the trail automatically. It has often been observed, particularly in laboratory colonies in 'observation nests', that a worker may be disturbed at one point and will then rush back to the rest of the colony executing the shaking movement every time it meets another termite. The termites it meets then tend to be drawn along the trail to the source of disturbance, and this is especially so for the soldiers.

Trail-laying has only recently been conclusively demonstrated in termites. Many people have found strong evidence that termites follow invisible trails. Earlier, Andrews[3] had managed to establish a 'short-circuit' of *Nasutitermes* workers around the edge of a prickly pear leaf. Goetsch did some interesting experiments with *Reticulitermes* clearly demonstrating that they mark the surface in some way. He waited for a trail to be established between a nest and a source of food, keeping the insects to a narrow path between two microscope slides. When the slides were moved to one side the termites still kept within the original limits of the path, even when the food was displaced relative to this. Goetsch also showed that where trails were at first devious they were gradually straightened out, and termites with more experience of a particular area took straighter paths. Andrews, in the West Indies, had found that the termites he was studying could still orientate correctly when walking across sand, even if he first disturbed the surface of the sand. This indicates that some termites may be able to make use of cues in their orientation other than the trail-laying that may be inferred. It could be that some species, like many species of ants, show a light compass orientation, in which they move keeping a constant angle with reference to the sun.

Goetsch[46] and others have suggested that the faecal particles and particles of wood and earth that mark termite trails are the real 'trail substances'. Grassé and Noirot[58] observed that *Odontotermes magdalenae*, an African termite that forages by day as well as by night, makes a sort of road (*chaussée pavée*) for itself. Tunnels from the nest open to the exterior some distance from it, and there is a circle of soldiers guarding the exit, with separate streams of termites entering and leaving the nest. Some of the workers leaving the nest carry with them a particle of earth moistened with saliva which is later deposited on the trail. Numerous particles become pressed down side by side so that eventually a fairly permanent paved roadway is formed 15–30 mm in diameter. The roads wind about for several dozen yards, branching when they approach the collecting area. The African *Trinervitermes,* which forage principally for grass seeds, produce a trail in a similar sort of way by the accumulation of droplets of excrement.

Stuart[156] in America and Lüscher and Müller[115] in Switzerland have investigated the trail-laying of termites in the laboratory. Working independently they were able to show that *Zootermopsis nevadensis* lays a discrete chemical trail. The Swiss workers found that after a termite had found its way to food in the form of moist sawdust it usually ran back to the rest of the colony with a particle of the sawdust between its jaws and appeared to alarm the others with the shaking movement. They began immediately to move around, most of them following very exactly the path taken by the first termite on its return journey. Of artificial trails made with water, wood extract, termite saliva, termite excreta, and homogenised termites, only the latter had an attraction for the termites. On painting over various segments (sternites) on the underside of the abdomen with lacquer it was found that the termites could lay an effective trail only when the area between the fourth and fifth sternites was left uncovered. The opening of a gland known as the sternal gland was found here. An ether extract of the gland is faithfully followed by the termites (Plate II), and the extract of one gland is sufficient for an effective trail of 50 m. A trail lasts for about half an hour, and is followed by termites walking on a gauze so that they cannot touch it with their feet or antennae. The trail substance which can clearly be regarded as a pheromone must therefore be detected by the termites as an odour.

Stuart experimenting with squashes of various parts of the body similarly traced the origin of the trail pheromone in both *Zootermopsis nevadensis* and *Nasutitermes cornigera* to the sternal gland. The latter species also lines its trail with faecal material, but this is clearly a secondary event since Stuart showed that the insects follow a freshly laid trail in preference to such an established trail.

It is interesting that the trail substances studied appear to have some specificity. The trail of *Zootermopsis nevadensis* also attracts the very closely related *Z. angusticollis,* but not the *Nasutitermes,* and an extract of the gland of *Kalotermes flavicollis* actually repelled *Z. nevadensis* individuals.[115] There appear to be at least two fractions to the trail substance, one of which is a powerful attractant and the other a chemical that confers specificity. Two separate chemicals have been identified in the trail of *Nasutitermes* by an Australian worker,[124] and an extract of the gland of *Zootermopsis* can be converted from a repellent to an attractant for *Kalotermes flavicollis* by heating. The trail pheromone of *Z. nevadensis* has very recently been subjected to chemical analysis.[95,98] Several components were identified, including a $C_{11}H_2O$ compound of low volatility, and hexanoic acid. The latter is highly volatile and extremely attractive to the termites: 1/50,000 of a milligram spread over a 10 cm trail with four 60° bends is followed by at least three out of ten termites. Other substances, such as citronellol and geraniol are also followed by the termites. Geraniol is an attractant produced by honeybees, but this is only half as effective for termites as hexanoic acid.

A rather odd finding has been that the ink of some ballpoint pens functions as a trail pheromone for some species of *Reticulitermes, Nasutitermes* and *Bulbitermes*.[10] The active ingredients have been identified as diethyleneglycol monobutane ether and diethyleneglycol monoethyl ether, both of which are also attractive to *Z. nevadensis* and *Z. angusticollis*. Also, wood decayed with the fungus *Lenzites trabea* is attractive to *R. flavipes* and *R. virginicus*. Analysis of extracts of the wood and of the trail glands of the termites has shown that both contain a substance, $C_{12}H_{19}OH$, which is very attractive to the termites when dissolved in hexane.[122]

The structure of the sternal gland has received some attention. There appears to be no duct associated with the glandular cells, but it seems likely that the secretion of the cells passes through fine pores in the cuticle to collect in a reservoir formed by the overlapping sternal plate of the preceding segment (see Fig. 10a). There are numerous campaniform sensilla, which are stress receptors, on the cuticle overlying the gland, and it has been suggested that when the abdomen is pressed against the ground these may regulate the degree of opening of the reservoir.[158]

Pasteels,[133] in a study of the trail formation by *Nasutitermes lujae* in the Gabon, found that among the two worker castes the older termites were the ones found most frequently on the trail. There was, as Fig. 10b illustrates, a corresponding development of the sternal gland. This division of labour within castes is sometimes called polyethism (ethology=the study of

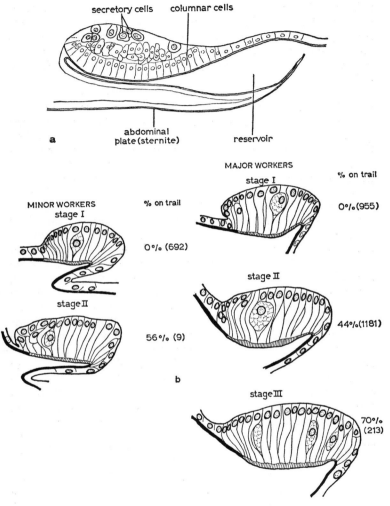

Fig. 10 (*a*) Longitudinal section through the sternal gland of *Zootermopsis nevadensis* (after Stuart[157]).

(*b*) Relative sizes of the sternal gland of different castes and instars of *Nasutitermes lujae*, seen in longitudinal section. The figures in brackets are the total numbers of each stage in samples taken in the nest and on the trail (after Pasteels[133]).

animal behaviour), in contrast to polymorphism. A similar
phenomenon is found in the honeybee, where in the worker there
is a corresponding growth in the size of the wax-secreting glands
on the abdomen and atrophy of the feeding glands in the head
as the workers change over the duties of feeding the brood and
building the comb.

Termites, like all other social insects, are attracted not only to
each other's trails but to each other, and Verron[159] in Paris has made
a detailed study of this inter-attraction. He had the insects walking
along a passage-way with a gauze floor above a series of tubes.
One tube contained a certain number of termites and the others
were filled with damp sand. Termites walking along the gauze
hesitated or stopped over the tube containing termites, and hence
measures could be made of the relative attractivity that different
castes held for others. It was found that generally the older the
termites in the tube the less attractive they were to the other
termites; thus the winged forms and the larvae and nymphs in
their last stages were least attractive. The search for the actual
substance involved in the inter-attraction revealed some interesting
facts: insects lose their attractive power when they are starved,
when they are deprived of their intestinal protozoa and can
therefore no longer digest wood and when they are fed on pure
cellulose. It seems evident that the attractive substance arises
from the digestion of wood. Verron extracted an active fraction
from *Kalotermes* nymphs and with the aid of Barbier,[160] a bio-
chemist, was able to show that this was an alcohol. Further
investigation was aided by the fact that the same substance
appeared to be present in the galleries constructed by *Microcerotermes edentatus,* which could be collected in reasonable quantity.
The substance turned out to be a form of hexenol; an alcohol
with six carbon atoms, which also occurs naturally in wood.
The hexenol was found to be strongly attractive to *Reticulitermes
lucifugus, R. flavipes, Nasutitermes* and *Microcerotermes* as well
as to *Kalotermes flavicollis.* One wonders, then, whether this is a
trail substance or pheromone of some sort. However, it would
be too early to jump to this conclusion since it is not attractive
to all termites and has different effects on *Zootermopsis* from
an extract of the sternal gland.

It is well known that social insects have their own nest odour.
This is composed of secretions on the surface of the cuticle and
odours adsorbed on to the cuticle from substances, such as food

materials, present in their own nest. If a termite enters the wrong nest its presence will be detected and it will be killed by members of that colony—this happens also between colonies of closely related species. They can be made to live together if they are first chilled in a refrigerator before they are mixed so that they are allowed to come to gradually in the presence of each other. The odours then have time to mix before the aggressive tendencies of the termites are aroused. In this way Dropkin[34] managed to establish mixed colonies of closely related species of *Kalotermes*. Emerson[35] mixed initially inimical colonies of *Nasutitermes banksi* by first mixing particles of wood and the nest materials and then shaking up the termites with the mixture.

The attraction of termites to each other finds its expression in relatively undisturbed conditions in trophallaxis, which has already been discussed, but when termites are suddenly disturbed as, for example, by opening their nest, trophallactic activity immediately ceases. The termites rush around, and when they meet other termites they make a rapid oscillatory movement, withdrawing by jerking backwards and then rocking forwards again. This behaviour will also occur when the termites touch any moving object, or an insect of another species. Analysis of ciné film shows that the withdrawal component occurs as soon as the antennae touch the object in question and then in the subsequent forward movement the terminal parts of the antennae are pressed against the object. There are numerous chemoreceptors on the segments of the antennae that are used here, and it seems that the termite makes a rapid 'chemical analysis' of the object and can thus determine whether it is an intruder or a nest-mate. If it meets a piece of cockroach cuticle, for example, it will then jerk back vigorously and run off in an agitated fashion, or alternatively, as do the soldiers particularly, attack the object.[88]

The insects most closely related to termites are the Blattaria or cockroaches. Jerking or rocking movements are often to be observed among these creatures. The American cockroach has a curious side-to-side rocking movement, the significance of which is unfortunately not clearly known. The same applies in the much more interesting case of the semi-social cockroach *Cryptocerus punctulatus*[25] which is reported to make the peculiar jerking movement characteristic of termites. This movement was observed to take place most often just before and during the breeding period. It is tempting to compare this with the situation in the Orthoptera (crickets and grasshoppers) where sound is used very commonly in attracting the sexes to each other as a preliminary to mating. It is a little-known fact that *Zootermopsis* winged forms have a tympanum on the abdomen in exactly the position of many grasshoppers and locusts. Tympana are completely unknown among cockroaches. This tympanum in *Zootermopsis* appears to be vestigial and non-functional, but its presence here suggests the possibility that airborne sound may have been used as a means of communication among ancestral termites. Vibration travels much better than airborne sound in the nests of present-day termites and this means of communication may have been abandoned early on as soon as the termites evolved their social way of life. This is not the only explanation, however, since tympanal organs are found in certain night-flying moths and are here used in detecting the high-pitched echolocation cries of bats.[138] The moths can then take various types of avoiding action if bats approach. The termite tympanum may therefore have been used by the winged forms in avoiding predators at a stage when the colony size of termites was relatively small and relatively few winged forms were produced. Winged forms are produced in present-day species in enormous numbers and so a proportion always manages to avoid predators.

Jerking movements are common in Orthoptera, and in the bush cricket, *Ephippiger bitterensis,* the male performs a movement of the body in a vertical plane consisting of about twenty-five oscillations over a period of about 1 second. This vibrates the foliage on which the insect is standing and guides the female to the male.[21] One wonders whether vibratory movements concerned with attraction of the sexes in the ancestors of termites may not have been taken over for the new function of social communication during the course of evolution. Jerking movements also occur in ants and they appear to transmit excitement to other ants. Recent studies on ant behaviour are demonstrating more and more the importance of pheromones in the organisation of the colony. Many of these pheromones are alarm substances and may be released during the jerking movements. It may well be that termites release alarm pheromones; so far only one has been detected, and it seems likely that the sticky secretion of *Nasutitermes* soldiers may contain an alarm substance. The trail substance appears to act both as an alarm substance and an attractant and the present evidence suggests that the jerking movement that is associated with trail laying is concerned only with mechanical excitation of other termites, but it does not mean that this is true for all species of termite. It is a peculiar fact that 'guests' or inquilines of termite colonies often perform jerking movements. Emerson observed a staphylinid beetle (*Termitogaster emersoni*) approach a *Nasutitermes* worker and jerk itself. The worker immediately started to lick the beetle, and when it stopped, further jerking promoted the licking. Here the question that Emerson posed in 1928 has still not been answered; since there was no contact between the two in this example is stimulation effected by the release of a pheromone?

The language of *Zootermopsis*, then, consists of jerking movements and trail-laying. Although there is no evidence for a language in the form of coding of taps, for example, one wonders whether something like this may exist in higher termites. This seems at first sight unlikely, since the tapping is a warning signal. There would not be much of value to the termites in coding this signal to indicate different sorts of predator, for example; even assuming the insects could discriminate between different kinds. If the activity of the termites is increased and at the same time they are dispersed into the deeper galleries this is probably the safest action against any intruder. It would even be difficult to have an 'all clear' signal that depended on tapping, since it would have to be very different from the warning signal if the possibility of confusion—with disastrous results no doubt—were not to exist. As it is, the termites continue tapping when disturbed and stimulate each other to tap. In the absence of any further disturbance they gradually 'run down' and so no all clear signal is necessary.

Where the discovery of a food source is being communicated, on the other hand, as in the dances of the honeybee, any coding of the information relative to direction, distance, etc., will have a large selective advantage since the success and survival of the colony could depend on information like this. In both ants and termites the odour trail performs the function of guiding workers to a food source or a source of disturbance very adequately without the need for the mediation of symbolic gestures or activities. The possibility remains nevertheless, that, in the mound-building termites in particular, other forms of communication exist. It certainly seems that the different castes have differing sensitivities to stimuli in these insects. The large soldiers of *Macrotermes* are quickly drawn to a source of disturbance while the workers and small soldiers retreat, the workers later appearing and repairing any breach in the nest wall. Behaviour like this could easily be explained in terms of differing thresholds to sensory stimuli among castes and the gradual adaptation of sense organs to sudden changes in conditions. In other words the soldiers are more 'highly strung' and show the same reactions to relatively small disturbances that the workers show to relatively large disturbances.

5

NESTS

The nests of termites include many remarkable, intricate and complex structures that are without parallel anywhere in the animal kingdom. The complexity of mound nests, for example, impressed biologists of the eighteenth and nineteenth centuries so much that they assumed without question that the creatures that built them must be highly intelligent and their society comparable in almost every way with human society. The first report to an English audience of the structure of the *Macrotermes* mound nests of Africa was given in 1781 by Henry Smeathman. Smeathman's imagination ran away with him more than a little, but his interpretation emphasises the difficulty of explaining how the behaviour of the termites is coordinated to produce complex structures. Nevertheless it is a tenet of modern biology that one should seek to explain animal behaviour in the simplest terms possible, and this implies an assumption that the behaviour is not the outcome of a higher mental faculty. The studies that have been made so far indicate that this approach is the correct one, as we shall see.

We have to thank two people in particular, Professors Grassé and Noirot, for the fact that we have a detailed knowledge of the structure of a wide range of types of termite nest, and much of the following account is based upon their descriptions. Grassé was originally a protozoologist who became fascinated by termites when he was investigating their intestinal protozoa, and as a professor at the Sorbonne has stimulated a great deal of research into termite biology throughout France in recent years.

There appears to have been much parallel evolution of nest structures among termites so that similar nests may be built by quite unrelated genera, and conversely, quite dissimilar nests may be built by closely related species of termite. Early workers made a classification of nests apart from the taxonomic classification of the insects, which in fact rather tends to complicate matters than simplify them. Nests were often divided into 'Non-concentrated nests' and 'Concentrated nests'[84]. The former variety were those that were not compact and consisted of an irregular system of galleries and chambers. Concentrated nests were divided by the Swedish scientist Holmgren into five different varieties. There were tree nests made out of 'wood carton', a chewed and partly digested wood pulp that dries quite hard, nests of wood and earth carton, nests of earth carton, mixed carton and earth nests and nests of earth only. Dr W. V. Harris in his book *Termites, their recognition and control*[72] makes the valuable point that the type of the nest depends largely on the feeding habits of the particular species. Thus the wood feeders make wood carton nests, surrounding these with a wall of earthen or wood and earth material when they are built on the ground. Soil feeding species mainly use their excreta which is fine clay and material of vegetable origin. Fungus-growing termites tend to use particular material such as sand that is around them, which is cemented together with clay or salivary secretions.

What we may reasonably assume to be the more primitive kinds of nest are found in the families *Kalotermitidae* and *Termopsidae*. The three species of *Zootermopsis*, which have often been used in laboratory studies, are found along the Pacific coastal region of the USA; colonies are usually found in decaying pine logs or felled trees, up to a level even above the snow line in winter. The 'nest' is a simple network of galleries, most of them running with the grain of the wood. These are the nests of damp-wood termites, but the species that do most damage to wooden buildings and installations are dry-wood termites. *Kalotermes flavicollis*, a dry-wood termite of southern Europe, often attacks the woody stems of vines, but not in sufficient numbers to be a serious pest. Anyone who has attempted to collect these termites by breaking open vine stems, even with the aid of a sharp axe, will admire their chewing efficiency. Again, galleries follow the grain of the wood, occasionally widening into larger cavities some of which are blind-ending pockets that serve as dumping grounds for faecal pellets. Before swarming time some galleries are extended upwards and outwards, serving as exit channels for the winged forms. In normal circumstances there are no openings to the exterior and the nest is isolated from the outside air. *Cryptotermes* species, on the other hand, make openings to the outside through which they eject their excreta, but they also have soldiers with phragmotic heads so that the exit holes can be closed up quickly and neatly. The holes may also be temporarily closed by a paper-like partition presumably made from partly digested wood.

Mastotermes darwiniensis from Australia, in other ways the most primitive of termites, strangely has behaviour more complex than any of the termites mentioned so far in this chapter. The nests are usually associated with living or felled trees, and consist, according to Hill,[78] of large horizontal cells filling the space that has been eaten out. Hill described a nest that developed under a fence support. Over a period of two years a network of galleries was built underground spreading over almost 100 m, and where these led to the surface the vegetation was covered with thick crusts of earthen building material under which the termites fed. In the interior of buildings, where conditions are relatively still and humid, *Mastotermes* builds delicate fern or leaf-like structures which may serve as ramps for extending the nest from one place to another. This insect can also build tunnel-like galleries through which it can pass from one tree to another without exposing itself to the outside air. It attacks some living trees in a peculiar way, producing what is called 'ring-barking'. It enters the tree below ground level, tunnels upwards for several feet and then outwards towards the cambium, making ring-shaped grooves in the trunk. The bark breaks away as the sap begins to escape, and the termites then ensheath several feet of the trunk with their building material.

The *Hodotermitidae*[27] are harvesters that build nests entirely underground in grassland or semi-desert areas. The nests of *Hodotermes mossambicus* found in the Transvaal are compact and almost spherical, divided into numerous chambers by horizontal and vertical partitions, most of which are filled with grass that has been collected. There are also galleries leading into cavities just around the nest where, again, collected grass is stored. The termites of this group have well-developed eyes and often forage in daylight in long trails, bringing back to the nest portions of the leaves of grasses and other plants which are first stored in cavities just below the surface. It is said that storing the grass here to begin with protects the young brood in the nest from the gases that are given off as the grass starts to ferment. The nests are found at depths of 1–3 m under the ground, occasionally much deeper, and the earth from the excavations is piled up in heaps above ground. The nests are interconnected with galleries where they come near to each other underground. In one area Dr Coaton found nine large nests all interconnected, only four of which contained young brood, so it was difficult to decide whether they could all be regarded as complete nests.

The nests of *Anacanthotermes*[50] are found in desert areas. Those in the Sahara consist of groups of irregular chambers, sometimes more than 1 m in diameter but rarely more than 1 cm high, interconnected by galleries. The uppermost chambers are filled with hay made from the germinating seeds of grasses and other plants.

The family Rhinotermitidae includes one of the few species found in Europe, *Reticulitermes flavipes*. It is essentially a damp-wood termite, but can be quite destructive in buildings where it finds warmth and moisture. It does, however, have the ability to make carton-like material, composed of wood, earth and faecal particles. This may be used for lining the galleries in the wood, building partitions in wood that they have eaten out, or for building tunnel galleries that extend out from the nest. By means of the latter they can bridge over substances that they are not very good at eating through, like concrete. This makes them more destructive creatures than *Zootermopsis*, for example, since they can extend their nest through the soil and can also extend their living quarters to the tops of trees or to the upper stories of buildings with their tunnel galleries. *Reticulitermes* species working in wood above damp earth sometimes extend galleries vertically downwards through the air for over three feet, possibly towards sources of moisture.

Psammotermes is a subterranean species that lives in steppe and desert regions, using as a building material sand cemented together with saliva. According to a description given by Dinter, (in *Die Termiten*[145]) in the nest of *Psammotermes allocerus* sand galleries may be found sticking above the surface, where the sand has been blown away by the wind. The nest itself consists of very flat chambers separated by thin horizontal floors. Around the

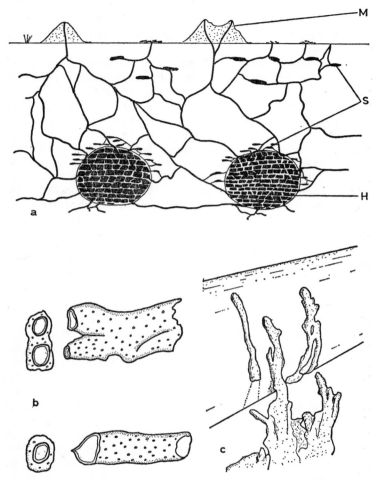

Fig. 11 (a) Section through the nest of *Hodotermes mossambicus* showing the nest proper, or hive (H), surrounded by storage cavities (S) for cut grasses, which are found again just below the surface of the soil. Small mounds (M) of excavated soil are often present (after Coaton[27]).

(b) Parts of suspended tunnel galleries constructed by *Reticulitermes flavipes* from a pine tree to the ground (after Banks and Snyder[5]).

(c) Tubular galleries constructed by *Reticulitermes* up to a furnace pipe (redrawn from a photograph by Light[102]).

nest are balloon-like spheres each containing a small heap of dry vegetable material with sand tubes leading vertically upwards from them.

The termites of the genus *Coptotermes* are important pests of living trees in Australia. *C. brunneus* builds large mounds which may be up to $2\frac{1}{2}$ m high and $1\frac{1}{2}$ m in diameter at the base. The mound is mainly unstructured clay, and the nest proper is made of carton and situated below ground. Greaves[66] has investigated another species, *C. acinaciformis,* in western Australia. The nest of these termites begins in tree trunks, but when the tree dies the colony may persist in a mound nest. Greaves traced the underground galleries emanating from nests of both species, and found that they were remarkably extensive. He located the galleries by digging around a nest and then followed them over short distances at a time by blowing coloured powder down them. In both species the maximum length was about 50 m. In one study, subterranean galleries from one colony were traced to fifteen living trees, as well as to dead trees, logs and stumps.

Coptotermes formosanus can construct nests of wood or faecal carton in the soil or in the wooden supports of buildings. *Schedorhinotermes* builds nests (Fig. 12*b*) that are very similar to those of *Coptotermes.*

Termites of the subfamily Nasutitermitinae are even more varied in the kinds of nest they build. *Trinervitermes*, for example, builds a peculiar nest consisting of a small dome of earth containing chambers, some of which are filled with hay or seeds. Cavities lead vertically down from this part of the nest to a much deeper part where most of the brood is to be found. Some Australian *Nasutitermes*[79] construct huge mound nests, of which perhaps the most remarkable are constructed by *N. triodiae*, a tropical species. Different kinds of nest are built by this insect in different areas, each area presumably being a different ecological zone. The 'Kimberley' type which attains a maximum height of nearly $4\frac{1}{2}$ m has overhanging sides or overlapping bulges giving the nest a unique and bizarre appearance. In some sandy areas large nests often occur surrounded by many smaller ones, which Hill suggests may be constructed by the progeny of the large nests. In other areas the so-called fluted or columnar nests occur, and these can occasionally attain the staggering height of nearly $7\frac{1}{2}$ m. According to Hill, again, the innermost galleries are used for disposal of the waste material of the colony, and sometimes become nesting places for enormous numbers of small black ants. There is no well-defined nursery, but the queen and brood are found at about ground level in the nest. The food consists of grass, which is cut in large quantities in the dry season and stored in peripheral chambers in the bulges or flutes.

Nasutitermes also build characteristic tree nests. One species (*N. ephratae*) seems to be an intermediate type since it normally

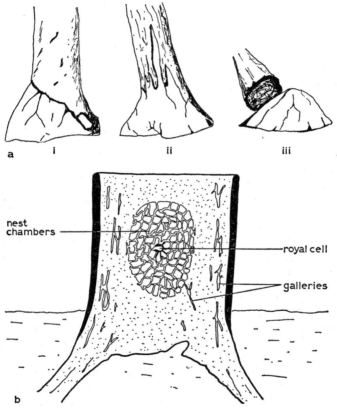

Fig. 12   (*a*) Stages in the development of a mound nest of *Coptotermes acinaciformis*. Clay is deposited around the base of a living tree (i), much clay is present around a dead tree (ii) and, finally, a domed mound forms at the end of an eaten out log (after Greaves[66]).

(*b*) Section through a nest of *Schedorhinotermes lamanianus* in an old tree trunk (after Grassé[50]).

builds tree nests in the Caribbean, but on grassland areas in Trinidad builds mound nests.[72] Some of the nests of mound-builders, like those of the Australian *N. exitiosus,* have the interior made predominantly of wood carton and the exterior mainly of inorganic material. Significantly, this species is one of the few Australian nasutes that attacks wood. Tree nests are usually fairly spherical, built around branches or in the forks of trees, and are made entirely of wood carton and covered with a thin friable layer. In Puerto Rico models of these nests are made out of concrete, painted black, and used as 'realistic' garden decoration.

Species of *Cornitermes*[51] are very common in South America. Although they are classed as nasutes they lack the nasute soldier and in this respect are considered primitive. They build mound nests originating, as do those of many *Nasutitermes,* around tree stumps or roots. In Brazil the clay they use for building the mounds is rich in mineral salts, such as aluminium and magnesium silicates with traces of iron, calcium, magnesium and sodium brought up from the surface of the rock strata below the soil. Some of the natives are known to include earth from the mound in their diet, much as more civilised people might take iron pills or liver salts, no doubt.

Amitermes has a wide distribution. In the USA some species cause extensive damage to vegetation or crops, which they usually cover with crusts of earthen material under which they feed.[5] Likewise, in Australia many species are more or less peripatetic, causing damage to vegetation and wood. But other species erect steep-sided mounds which are often locally very abundant, making some areas look like cemeteries. Occasionally there is a tendency for mounds to be longer in the N-S axis, and this feature is particularly strong in the remarkable nests of the compass or magnetic termites (*Amitermes meridionalis*—'one of the phases of termite life which tax human belief' as Professor A. E. Emerson put it. These nests are roughly square viewed from east or west (Fig. 14), reaching a height of about 4 m. Viewed from the north or south they are roughly triangular and about 1 m wide at the base, which is the widest part. The long axis is always directed north–south. It has been suggested that the orientation is an adaptation to avoid damage in gales or to allow for rapid drying of new constructions during the wet season. A more likely explanation is that the nest form aids temperature regulation. The smallest angle will be presented to the sun when

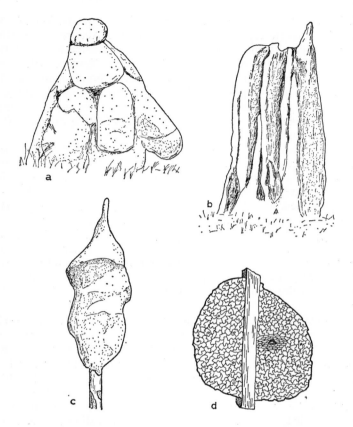

Fig. 13 (*a*) and (*b*) Two types of nest mound built by *Nasutitermes triodiae* in Australia. Both are about 5 m high, but the columnar type (*b*) may reach a height of 8 m.

(*c*) Nest of a species of *Nasutitermes* over 2 m high, surmounting a post in Brazil.

(*d*) Section through a nest of *Nasutitermes arborum*. The royal cell can be seen but the friable outer layer of the nest is not shown.

(*a*) and (*b*) from photographs in Hill[79], (*c*) from a photograph in Gonçalves and Silva[47], and (*d*) after Grassé[50].

it is at its hottest, at midday, the maximum irradiation will be obtained when the sun's power is lowest. According to Hill, some tropical termite species move to the warmest side of the nest during the winter: to the east in the morning and the west in the afternoon. He believes that the meridional nests may be adapted to this requirement. Whatever the precise significance of the compass mounds, the question of how the insects manage to build them in this form is the most fascinating one, and this will be discussed again.

Many species of *Amitermes* feed on vegetable material such as seeds, grass, and decaying material. This is stored in the outer galleries of the mound, and it is reported that in some species masses of dead termites are stored in the upper parts of the nest and that these also appear to be food stores (as well as cemeteries, one might add). The related *Globitermes* from south-east Asia[130] builds a nest that is more complex than those of the Australian *Amitermes* internally (Fig. 14). It has a thin outer covering of earthen material which is supported on small conical pillars of the wall underneath. The wall itself has an outer zone with relatively large galleries and chambers and an inner zone with smaller galleries.

A central space contains large balls of triturated vegetable material, some up to 7 cm in diameter, which appear to be food reserves, but in their structure they foreshadow the fungus gardens of the mound-building higher termites. Below this is a zone consisting of fine carton lamellae which form leaf-like chambers, and embedded in this is a compact nodule which contains the royal cell—a complex nest, that is even more remarkable for the fact that it is built with three different materials Earthen material predominates in the outer layers; excremental material gradually increases in content towards the central zones, where there is also a relatively large content of undigested vegetable material.

The fungus-growers, or Macrotermitinae, build the largest nests of all: the 'ant hills' that are so well known in Africa and which Smeathman described. Many different forms of nest are found, but they are all characterised by the numerous cavities containing fungus gardens, which are tortuously sculptured balls of vegetable material supporting fungi upon which the termites graze. The one exception to this appears to be *Sphaerotermes sphaerothorax* which is found in the Congo.[55] The nest consists of interconnected subterranean spheres placed around the roots of trees or bushes. Each sphere has an air space around it. There is a thick outer wall of clayey earth with a large central cavity transversed by a dense tangle of roots amongst which numerous fungus gardens are to be found. Surprisingly these 'fungus gardens' are completely sterile and their function can only be guessed at. A cyst-like inward growth of the nest wall contains the royal chamber which opens into two other chambers in the nest wall.

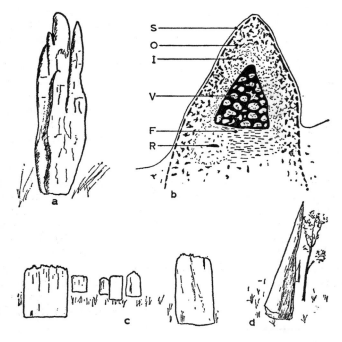

Fig. 14 (a) Mound nest of *Amitermes vitiosus*, about 2 m high.

(b) Section through a mound of *Globitermes sulphureus* showing the outer shell (S), outer (O) and inner (I) zones of the wall, balls of vegetable material (V), flat, thin-walled carton chambers (F) and the royal cell in a clay nodule (R).

(c) Mounds of the compass termite, *Amitermes meridionalis*, viewed from the eastern aspect. (d) Mounds viewed from the southern aspect. The mounds are about 4m high.

(a), (c), and (d) drawn from photographs in Hill[79], (b) after Noirot[130].

Many Macrotermitinae build underground nests which do not develop into mounds and are therefore difficult to find. An example is *Syncanthotermes*, which like *Sphaerotermes*, builds a nest consisting of a number of separate subspherical units interconnected by galleries (Fig. 15).

Usually, piles of chewed wood and other vegetable material are stored close to the fungus gardens, which are themselves made largely out of partly digested wood. *Syncanthotermes* is apparently exceptional in not having these piles of 'sawdust'. *Pseudacanthotermes spiniger* has a similar sort of underground nest, but before swarming takes place domes are built above ground which apparently serve as towers from which winged termites launch themselves.

Many species of *Protermes* and *Odontotermes* have somewhat similar nests, but chimneys are built projecting above the ground level. These are the openings of large ducts that penetrate below the ground to the region of the fungus gardens. Grassé and Noirot[61] insist that in no cases do the ducts open directly to the fungus gardens, but are blind-ending so that there is no possibility, contrary to the suggestions of earlier termitologists, that currents of air are set up that ventilate the nest. Certainly, there appears to be great variability of form among the nests of these termites. Some have nests like *Syncanthotermes* with no ducts, others have large ducts leading off from the cavities containing fungus gardens but which are entirely below ground and do not open to the surface at all. *Odontotermes obesus* from the Himalayas builds large fluted mounds like those of some of the Australian nasutes but they contain large ducts which, again, do not open to the outside air. In South Africa, however, Coaton[26] has described the nests of three species of *Odontotermes* that appear to be quite unlike those found anywhere else. The nest of one

---

Fig. 15 (*a*) Section through part of a nest of *Sphaerotermes sphaerothorax* built in soil around the base of a tree. The central cavity contains galleries and fungus gardens among roots. Thick connections run to similar spheres.

(*b*) Section through a nest of *Syncanthotermes heterodon*, consisting of 7 units, the central one of which contains the royal cell.

(*c*) Section through a nest of *Pseudacanthotermes spiniger* showing cavities with fungus gardens below ground level and above ground an emergence tower for winged forms.

(*a*) after Grassé and Noirot[55], (*b*) and (*c*) after Grassé and Noirot[59].

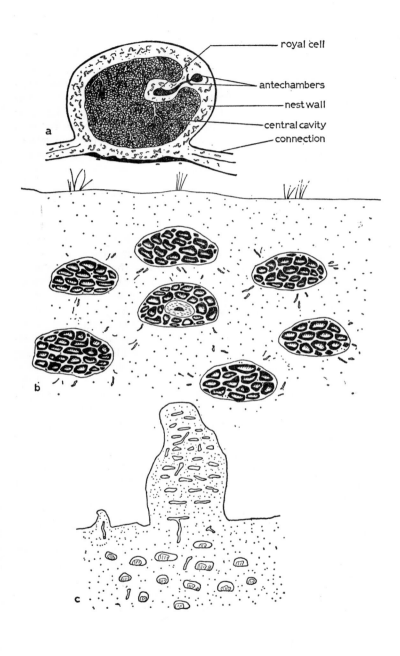

example he investigated (*O. transvaalensis*) had several chimneys, the tallest of which was 1·3 m high. These and other smaller openings led down directly to supplementary fungus chambers, which Coaton says ranged in size from that of a football to that of a large potato. These chambers were connected with each other and with the central part of the nest by passageways. The main cavity contained strata of fungus gardens separated by thin clay floors. There seems no doubt here that the living quarters of the termites are in direct contact with the outside air, since Coaton reports that if a chimney is broken off it is sometimes possible to see a fungus garden by shining a torch down the hole. The central cavity of the nest, however, is connected with the large ducts only indirectly through the fungus chambers. Chimneys have sometimes been found sealed off inside with an earthen partition built by the termites. This seems to hint that the termites regulate the passage of air into the nest under certain conditions.

It is termites of the genus *Macrotermes* that build the most conspicuous mound nests[63]. The simplest forms consist of more or less densely packed fungus chambers within a mound which also contains very many large branching galleries, which, although they sometimes connect up with the fungus chambers do not open to the outside air. In other species, such as *Macrotermes ivorensis,* the fungus chambers are all built on to one another, forming a compact central part around which there is an air space. A nest on a somewhat similar plan is built by *Macrotermes bellicosus.* As is generally the case, the nest first develops below ground as a large fungus garden divided by irregularly branching partitions and containing the royal cell in the centre. As the nest increases in size the termites build a dome above ground level and then the fungus gardens are removed from the central nest cavity as new ones are gradually set up in separate chambers outside the original confines of the nest. Above ground level, more domes are built around the original one but these are gradually worn down by erosion so that a gently sloping hillock is eventually formed. The older nests can be gigantic: up to nearly 6 m high and 30 m in diameter. In equatorial Africa they dominate the landscape in some regions and may obtain a density of about four nests per acre. Grassé and Noirot note that these hillocks, covered with tall plants and even scrub, confer an extremely peculiar character on the savanna, which (in their opinion) is without parallel on this planet.

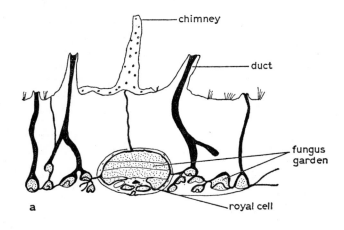

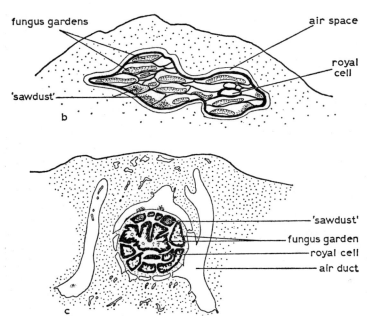

Fig. 16 (a) Section through a nest of *Odontotermes transvaalensis*.
(b) Section through a nest of *Macrotermes ivorensis*.
(c) Section through a young nest of *Macrotermes natalensis*.
(a) After Coaton[26], (b) after Grassé and Noirot[59], (c) after Grassé[50].

The termite *Macrotermes bellicosus* is quite variable in its habits throughout different parts of Africa. In many parts of north-western Africa nests are predominantly below ground level and only rarely are domes or towers found projecting above the ground. They generally have a diffuse internal structure, as does the nest of *M. goliath*, with groups of fungus chambers well separated from one another. Madame Bodot has studied the growth of these nests in the Ivory Coast and confirmed that they develop mainly in a horizontal direction from their initial almost spherical form. The air space around the internal nest also disappears as the nest increases in size.

Mounds with a different internal structure are built by *Macrotermes natalensis,* which is common through Africa. The mounds are very striking structures, and come in assorted shapes which may vary according, perhaps, to the local climate, soil conditions, and shelter given by vegetation. Possibly there are also different races with slightly different building habits. On open grassland the mounds tend to be more rounded and dome shaped, but where the cover is better the towers above ground may be quite narrow and resemble chimneys or cathedral spires, or, as in the Ivory Coast have numerous thick and prominent 'ribs' on the outside.

As the nest develops the fungus chambers remain closely associated forming a compact structure sometimes called the hive. The air spaces are not lost but develop around the hive giving rise to ascending ducts in the young nest. An extensive system of ducts is found in the 'adult' nest, permeating the wall and opening into the air space around the hive. There is some argument about where these ducts go, as we shall see later.

It may be thought that the *Macrotermes* mound nests represent the pinnacle of industrial achievements for the insect world. This must be so. According to my approximate calculations, if termites were the size of men, the largest nest they would build would be about a mile high—four times the height of the Empire State building—and five miles in diameter. What a tedious operation! Nevertheless, ant-eaters on the same scale would be 200–300 m long, so a structure of this proportion might not be so pointless as it may seem at first sight. But there are termites that build much more delicate nests that are in their way just as impressive, as the giant mounds. *Procubitermes* builds nests on tree trunks and above the nest builds a series of ridges, each in the shape of an inverted V, that are believed to divert rainwater running down the trunk away from the nest. *Cubitermes intercalatus* which Professor Emerson[36] studied in the Congo, goes further and builds a series of overlapping brackets on tree trunks, something like bracket fungi, which appear to form very effective multi-storey umbrellas for the nest. *Cubitermes* species that are found in grassland areas frequently build mushroom-shaped nests, especially in regions of heavy rainfall, but in dry areas they tend to build small mounds without an umbrella cap—which would seem to demonstrate rather clearly that it is an umbrella and not a sun-shade.

The most delicate and beautiful nests of all are those of the genus *Apicotermes*, which are probably the most finely engineered structures built in the animal world (see Plate III). The nests are, roughly speaking, eggshaped and are found about one foot below ground on average. They are often found in sandy soil and may be surrounded by an air space. They have been found most commonly in the Congo basin, but a relatively primitive species has been found in South Africa by Dr Coaton. This species (*A. trägårdhi*) has quite a simple nest consisting of a short series

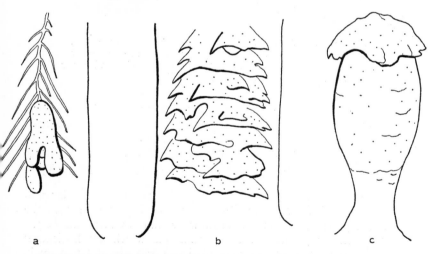

a   b   c

Fig. 17   (a) Nest of *Procubitermes sierraleonicus* on a tree trunk.
(b) Nest of *Cubitermes intercalatus* on a tree trunk (after Emerson[36]).
(c) Nest of *Cubitermes fungifaber* (about 60cm high).

D

of spirally wound chambers.[148] A nest of somewhat greater complexity is built by *A. rimulifex*,[33] which was found by accident when a trench was being dug in Katanga. 12 to 13 cm high, the nest was covered with a thin so-called 'shagreen' layer of granular sandy material. The outside of the nest proper had a large number of raised tubercles each containing a rectilinear

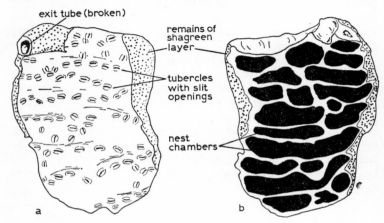

Fig. 18 (*a*) Lateral view of the nest of *Apicotermes rimulifex* with the shagreen layer largely removed. (*b*) The same nest in vertical section. The large chambers communicate through small openings. (Drawn from photographs by Desneux[33]).

slit-shaped opening communicating directly with the chambers inside the nest. Dr Jules Desneux, who described this nest, remarks that the precision of form of each of the slits is so great as to give the impression of the work of a machine tool. The large chambers within the nest are joined in ascending series by spiral galleries.

Nests of the more advanced species are more regular and symmetrical in structure.[146,147] The openings which may be either pores or slits are arranged in regular rows and may open only indirectly into the inner chambers which are horizontal and parallel storeys separated by floors only about 1 mm thick. 'Staircases' join the floors. In some species these are simple ramps with holes at each floor level and in others they are effectively spiral staircases with holes and curved pillars directly above one another. At the top of the nest are usually several upwardly projecting ledges with openings at their bases which are exit ramps for the termites.

The structures of the pores or slits varies from species to species and has been used for classifying the termites.[38] They are, after all, the expression of instinctive behaviour patterns of the insects which must be inherited genetically like any feature of body structure, but in the same way it must be remembered that they can be modified by the effects of environment. Professor Konrad Lorenz has aptly called *Apicotermes* nests 'frozen behaviour'.

A. lamani nests have openings that are almost bottle-shaped (see Fig. 19). In the majority of species the pores or slits open into circular galleries in the nest wall that run right round the circumference of the nest, but those of *A. occultus* are peculiar

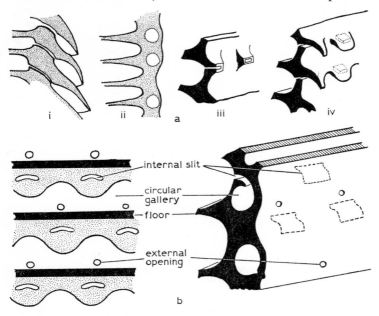

Fig. 19 (*a*) Sections of the nest wall in *Apicotermes lamani* (i), *A. occultus* (ii), *A. gurgulifex* (iii), and *A. desneuxi* (iv).

(*b*) Radiograph of the nest wall (left) and section of the nest wall (right) of *A. kisantuensis*.

(*a*) (i) and (ii) after Weidner in Schmidt[145], remainder after Schmidt[146,147].

in that there are no external openings to the circular galleries: this was assumed to be a distinct species before the termites had been collected with the nests.

Nests of another group show a series in the development of circular galleries. In *A. gurgulifex* the slits open directly through 'gargoyles' on the outside of the nest. The next stage is seen in *A. desneuxi* in which the slits open under downward projecting lips, and in one nest that has been collected, unfortunately without the termites, the lips curve right round and fuse with the wall at their ends to make short lengths of circular galleries.

In *A. kisantuensis* the slits open into complete circular galleries, and these open to the exterior through regularly placed pores which alternate in position with the slits.

Both the internal slits and the external pores of the nest are too small for the termites to pass through them. It seems most likely that their function is to allow the exchange of gases. Carbon dioxide will tend to build up in concentration inside the nest through the respiration of the termites and this will diffuse out through the openings in the nest wall as oxygen will diffuse in. It has been suggested that the circular galleries help to prevent the direct seepage of soil water into the nest and also make it difficult for insects that attack termites to enter the nest. If other insects were able to enter the nest at any point, the nest floor on which they found themselves could easily be sealed off by the soldiers blocking the small holes communicating between the floor levels.

It is only in the group containing, amongst others, *A. gurgulifex, desneuxi,* and *kisantuensis* that the nest is surrounded by a layer of sand and not by an air space. Father Bouillon in Leopoldville has recently been able to study excellent *Apicotermes* material.[15] He suggests that the sand, which is white and coarse, could be a residue left after the termites have extracted suitable building material. He also suggests that the saturated hot air produced by the metabolism of the termites in the enclosed space could diffuse out of the nest openings and condense in the cooler soil around the nest. The main constituents of the soil would then be leached away over the course of time leaving the coarse sand. The sand itself, of course, would drain well and retain air around the nest.

Unfortunately, we know only too little about the ecology of these fascinating termites. It would be very interesting to know how the distribution of nests was limited by the permeability of the soil, whether the nests could survive waterlogging for short periods, and so on. At the present we can only guess at the significance of the nest structure, until further studies are made. Bouillon, whose work is adding greatly to our knowledge of these termites, found that *A. gurgulifex* was a savanna species, while *A. desneuxi* and *kisantuensis,* building more complex nests, were forest species. But the picture as a whole for *Apicotermes* seems rather confusing; indeed, Dr de Barros Machado in Angola has questioned whether some of the species described are genuine, since the classification has sometimes been based mainly on features of the nest that he has found are, in fact, quite variable.[117]

It is where termites have become independent of living or dead trees for food that their nests have become most complex and their societies largest. Societies of *Zootermopsis angusticollis* in decaying wood number only about 2,000 individuals, and this is probably also an average figure for many dry-wood termites like *Kalotermes flavicollis.* Termites that have developed the ability to extend their nests and feeding areas by tunnel galleries tend to have larger colonies, like *Reticulitermes* colonies which may have up to half a million individuals. Insects like these have no nest in the true sense, but termites with a greater feeding range, like the nasutes have a permanent nest from which they forage. These nests may contain several million termites. A nest studied by Andrews in Jamaica had a population of about half a million with a maximum of 8,000 termites leaving the nest an hour on foraging expeditions[3]. Mound nests can also support large populations in suitable areas. There have been estimated to be 1,806,500 termites in a mound nest of *Nasutitermes exitiosus* and about two million in large nests of *Macrotermes natalensis.* Termites have become much more independent of the environment with the development of the mound-building habit, especially where this includes fungus feeding, and various devices are present to ensure constant conditions within the nest.

The fungus-growing habit, connected with the concentration of a large population in a small area means that the replenishment of air and the regulation of temperature become serious problems. Termites, as we shall see, can probably overcome these problems in mound nests, but in other cases they appear to have avoided them neatly by having nests that are not concentrated but are spread out over a large area underground, as in various members

D*

of the *Acanthotermes* group, for example, where fungus gardens
are in separate interconnected chambers. In many such species
with diffuse underground nests it is often difficult to say what are
the limits of a single nest. Even in some *Apicotermes* adjacent
nests appear to be in communication and there is sometimes only
one royal couple for several nests. This, however, appears to be
a coming together rather than a splitting up of nests, since
Bouillon has found what are clearly fused nests.

Mixed nests of termites often occur among some species. Some
of the species of *Amitermes* in Australia that exist in small colonies
under stones and in dead trees may also occasionally be found
in the nests of other species. The African termite *Pseudacanthotermes militaris* commonly builds within the mounds of other
termites, such as *Cubitermes* and *Amitermes*. It takes over existing
chambers, enlarges them, and divides them up by horizontal
partitions but never mixes with the 'host' termites. This habit
may often be confusing to the taxonomist; indeed, this goes for
termite nests as a whole, which may be considerably modified
by ecological conditions and so give rise to the idea that different
species are present in different areas.

6

NEST CLIMATE AND NEST-BUILDING

Constant conditions are maintained in the hive of the honeybee by many remarkable adaptive mechanisms in the behaviour of the bees and in the structure of their hive. The hive temperature is maintained between 34·5° and 35·5°C in the nursery area. If this temperature falls, the bees cluster, concentrating the heat produced by their metabolism. If the temperature rises, they fan at the hive entrance, producing a cooling draught of air, and some individuals fetch water which is spread on to the combs and cools them as it evaporates. It is less well known that similar homeostatic mechanisms are found among termites, and in some respects they make honeybees look mere amateurs as far as maintenance of a stable climate within the nest is concerned.

Nest humidity

Many species of termite exist where there is an annual very long dry season. Grassé and Noirot[54] found that *Cubitermes* in West Africa vacated the above-ground section of their nest during the dry season and went below-ground where the soil had a higher moisture content. Other termites, such as *Macrotermes bellicosus,* keep the humidity of the nest high, at least in the nursery area, by using a method similar to that of the honeybees—secreting watery saliva or watery crop contents on to the material of the nest. *Psammotermes,* which lives in the dry desert sand of the Sahara manages, rather astonishingly, to maintain a high humidity in its nest even though there is very little water content in the food it eats. Individual termites actually go down to the water table—

which may lie at a depth of up to 40 m—and bring up moist particles with which they 'humidify' the nest.

The relative humidity (R.H.) in termite nests is usually very high. Lüscher took measurements in the nests of five species in the Ivory Coast which built different types of nest (Fig. 21) and found that the R.H. was usually between 98 and 99% and never dropped below 96·2% irrespective of the outside temperature. In 1938 two Australians, Fyfe and Gay,[45] in a very interesting but surprisingly little-known study, brought to light some phenomena that ensure humidity control in the mound nest of *Nasutitermes exitiosus* (Fig. 20). The mound consists of three regions: an outer wall, an inner wall, and a central nursery. Measurements on four mounds showed that the R.H. of the nursery area was between 96 and 98% while the temperature of the outer wall varied between 11·4° and 36·8°C. The proportion of organic material in each region decreased from a maximum in the nursery area to a minimum in the outer wall, and the capacity for absorbing moisture was related to the relative amount of organic material present. Thus at a given temperature, the nursery material could adsorb about twice as much moisture as the outer wall (Fig. 20). This has functional importance, because if all parts of the mound had equal adsorbencies it would mean that, with a fall in outside temperature, moisture would accumulate in the outer wall by condensation and would tend to be lost by evaporation. However, as the nursery material is actually more hygroscopic it sets up a humidity gradient which reverses the effect of the temperature gradient and so conservation of moisture is achieved.

A dangerous situation could arise for the termites if the outer wall heated to the same temperature as the nursery (about 36°C) with the nest atmosphere near saturation. If the outside temperature fell, the moisture content of the nursery area might eventually reach saturation and the termites would be overwhelmed by condensation. This, it seems, cannot actually happen because of the different water-vapour pressures set up by the nest materials. Thus if the outside pressure fell to 26°C, the vapour pressure in the outer wall would fall to about 25 mm (Fig. 20). Since the temperature in the nursery is usually maintained around 36°C the vapour pressure there would remain high (44 mm). There would therefore be a movement of moisture along this gradient towards the outer wall, so that saturation would not occur in the nursery area.

Mounds can fairly effectively resist the threat of heavy rain-storms. Their outer crust is made of an impervious layer of sand and clay particles cemented together with the termites' salivary secretion. Water also diffuses extremely slowly through the nest material which has a high content of colloidal material; and the movement of water vapour is impeded by the tortuous nature of the galleries.

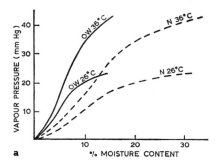

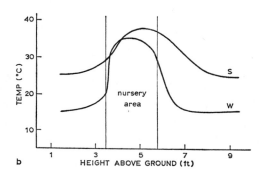

Fig. 20 (a) Moisture adsorption isothermals at 26°C and 36°C for nest material of *Nasutitermes exitiosus*. N, nursery; OW, outer wall.

(b) Temperature through the centre of a colony of *Coptotermes acinaciformis* in a blackbutt tree on a summer (S) and on a winter (W) day. The greater steepness of the winter curve is a reflection of greater aggregation of the termites.

(a) after Fyfe and Gay[45], (b) after Greaves[67].

Nest temperature

Mechanisms for temperature stabilisation have also been found
in this same species. The climate in the nest is sufficiently equable
for Monitor lizards to lay their eggs there occasionally, although
this habit is more prevalent in the Nile Monitor, *Varanus niloticus,*
which lays its eggs in the mounds of *Nasutitermes trinervoides*
in Natal.

Over a period of three days, the nursery temperature of one
mound of *N. exitiosus* fluctuated by about 2–3°C while the
temperature of the north wall of the mound dropped by about 12°C
during the night[82]. The temperature of the nursery area varied
during the year, falling by about 15°C to a minimum in the
winter months. There was evidence for a buffering effect to sudden
falls of temperature resulting from the termites returning from
outer areas to the centre of the mound. This effect has also been
seen in nests of *Coptotermes* in living trees.[67] Here the tree provides effective insulation for the termite just as the mound wall
does for other species. In *C. acinaciformis* the nursery temperature varied from 33° to 38°C throughout the year, and it was kept
at the high level during the winter by the termites gradually
reducing the volume of the living space (Fig. 20)—a similar
phenomenon to the clustering of honeybees.

In his study of Ivory Coast nests, Lüscher[114] found a number
of devices which contributed to temperature regulation in the
nests of different species. The nest of *Amitermes* is fairly spherical,
built in the shade or in the open, and consists of irregular thin-
walled cavities connected by narrow passages. Fluctuations in
internal temperature here are nearly as great as those in external
temperature (Fig. 21). *Thoracotermes macrothorax* builds similar
but columnar nests in the forest shade where the environmental
temperature fluctuates very little so that the problem of regulation
is avoided and no special modifications of nest structure for
insulation are present. The thick outer wall of *Cephalotermes*
nests, combined with location in a shady place, often around
tree bases, results in a fairly constant temperature in the nest.
(Fig. 21). Lüscher found the greatest degree of homeostasis in
the mound nest of *Macrotermes natalensis* (Fig. 21). Here, the
wall of the nest is up to two feet thick and forms a very effective
insulation.

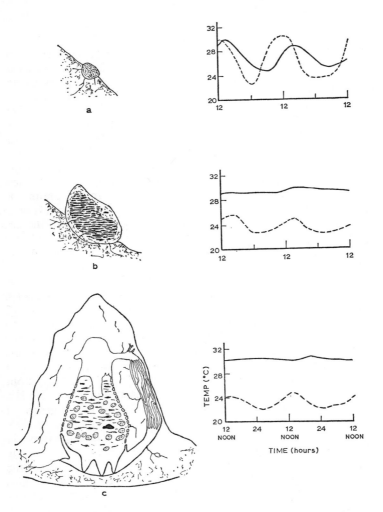

Fig. 21 Internal temperatures of the nests of *Amitermes evuncifer* (*a*), *Cephalotermes rectangularis* (*b*), and *Macrotermes natalensis* (*c*), taken over a period of two days. Continuous line, inner temperature; broken line, external temperature. (After Lüscher[114]).

Air conditioning

The greater the insulation and isolation of the termites from the outside environment, the greater must become the problems of gas exchange. It is known that termites can survive in unusually high concentrations of carbon dioxide. The concentration of CO_2 above ground level in an area in Kinshasa inhabited by *Cubitermes intercalatus* was 0·03%, but reached 0·92% in parts of the nest.[39] Experiments have shown that *Zootermopsis nevadensis* could respire normally in an atmosphere of 20% CO_2. *Nasutitermes exitiosus* will exist in the laboratory without CO_2, but it has been suggested that the build-up of the gas in the nest is responsible for the termites opening holes in the mound at certain times. The size of the ventilation hole in a colony kept in a jar varied according to fluctuations in the CO_2 level in the jar. High oxygen tensions will actually kill *Reticulitermes flavipes*,[17] but this effect is reduced when the oxygen is mixed with carbon dioxide.

Lüscher[110] pointed out that even allowing for this tolerance, gas exchange would present a very acute problem in nests such as those of *Macrotermes*. He calculated that if a large mound of *M. natalensis* contains about 2 million termites, amounting to about 20 kilograms of insects, and that these use about 500 cubic mm of oxygen per gram per hour (figures based on measurements on *Kalotermes* and *Zootermopsis*), then they would require about 1,200 litres of air per day. However, the nest contains only about 500 litres and if this is isolated the termites would survive for less than twelve hours. The carbon dioxide content in the centre of the nest was found by Lüscher to be only 2·7%, so that clearly there must be some means of renewing the air in the mound.

The *Macrotermes natalensis* nests in the Ivory Coast are heavily fluted, with prominently projecting 'ribs' on the outer wall of the mound. These contain part of an air duct system, which begins near the top of the nest as six to twelve radial canals, the thickness of a man's arm, pass into the top of the ribs and, as they descend, divide into smaller branches two to three cm in diameter. At about ground level they reunite to form ducts 10–15 cm thick which open below the nursery area in the cellar region. The microclimatic measurements that Lüscher took at various points in this system demonstrated the existence of an air circulation based on convection currents (Fig. 22).

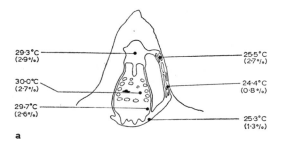

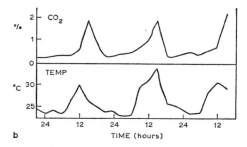

Fig. 22 (*a*) Measurements of temperature and carbon dioxide content (in brackets) in a mound of *Macrotermes natalensis* in the Ivory Coast.

(*b*) Carbon dioxide levels in the hive and temperatures in the soil 20 cm below ground near a mound of *Macrotermes natalensis* at Kinshasa.

(*a*) after Lüscher[110,114], (*b*) after Ruelle[140].

The activity of the termites in the central area warms the air and raises the CO_2 content. The air rises to the upper air space (the attic) and is then forced out by the slight excess pressure generated through the radial ducts into the ribs. These act as lungs: carbon dioxide diffuses out through the thin walls of the ribs and oxygen diffuses in. The ducted air is cooled in the same process and sinks so that at the bottom of the ribs the air that is funnelled to the cellar has the lowest temperature and CO_2 content.

Differences exist among the nests of *Macrotermes natalensis* in different geographical regions. Whether this is because some aspects of the nest form are dictated by certain ecological conditions, as appears to be the case in some species of *Apicotermes,* or whether the regional differences reflect termites that are genetically different (subspecies perhaps) is not known. The Uganda nests of *M. natalensis* have smooth walls without the projecting ribs and in correlation with this the air circulation system is on a different pattern. The warm air rises into the attic, as before, but from here ducts lead the air upwards into large but shallow apical cavities that lie just below the surface of the mound. The air pressure resulting from the rising currents forces air through the porous wall. Pressure is therefore low at the base of the mound where, as a result, air enters through large ducts that communicate between the cellar and the outside air. There are conflicting accounts of the structure of the East African nests and a wide and thorough survey would be of great value, but at least in some regions basal holes in the nest are consistently seen, and in others, for example in regions of Ethiopia, the mound is relatively chimney-shaped and open at the top.

The nests in the region of Kinshasa have formed the subject of an excellent and detailed study by Father Ruelle.[140] They appear in many ways to be intermediate between the Ivory Coast and Uganda types: the young mounds are more like the former and the old mounds more like the latter. In order to demonstrate the air duct system in a nest, Ruelle poured in over 800 lb of Portland cement to fill the air passages and then chipped away the nest material. The astonishing reticulated sculpture that resulted is shown in Plate IV.

The concrete skeleton showed that the attic connected with ascending galleries, and that the radial ducts connecting the hive with the periperal vertical ducts were very numerous and were present at various levels down to ground level. The periperal ducts united below this to give enormous conduits that opened into the cellar about 50 cm below soil level. In attempts to demonstrate the 'thermosiphon' effect described by Lüscher, Ruelle took measurements in the nest with a manometer sensitive to pressure changes of the order of 2×10^{-6} atmospheres, but

---

Plate III

    (a) Side view of a subterranean nest of *Apicotermes gurgulifex.*
    (b) Sectional half of a 'twin' nest of *Apicotermes arquieri,* formed
by fusion of two original nests.
Both about half natural size.

PLATE III

(a)

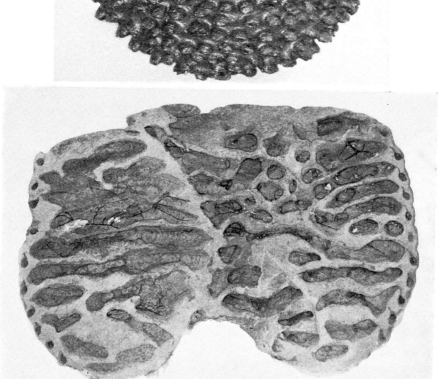

(b)

PLATE IV

Concrete 'skeleton' of the air-duct system in a mound nest of
Macrotermes natalensis. (Reproduced by permission of J. E. Ruelle.)

was unable to detect any pressure differences. That convection currents do exist, a fact disputed by Grassé and Noirot[61], was made evident by the current of warm humid air that issued when one of the pinnacles of the mound was decapitated. Further, measurements with a sensitive anemometer have conclusively confirmed that there is air flow within the mound. There is a 'steady state' flow of air at roughly the rate which Lüscher calculated must be present, i.e. 12 cm per minute. This flow is in an upward direction in the attic and, at least in the mornings, in a downward direction in the peripheral ducts leading to the cellar. The flow in the ducts, however, may reverse in direction during the day, possibly because of local heating effects. A further complicating factor is the wind, which superimposes irregular 'gusts' of air movement on the steady state régime. These short-lived gusts have velocities of up to 2 m per minute.

Father Ruelle's studies on Kinshasa nests of the 'Ivory Coast' type showed that heat production in the hive keeps the temperatures there at a mean value of about 30°C. This mean varies less than half a degree throughout the year, although fluctuations may exceed 3°C on particular days. The carbon dioxide concentration in the hive averages about 0·6% in the dry season but rises to about double this in the rainy season. The concentration follows a circadian rhythm (Fig. 22) which is detectable in the ducts and the cellar, as well as in the hive, from which one must conclude that there is air circulation within the mound. The CO_2 concentration in the hive is greatly affected by air currents outside the hive and by the effects of rain. It may be added that some kind of humidity control similar to that of *Nasutitermes exitiosus* can be presumed to exist here also, since it has been found that the outer wall is made of earth pellets cemented together with saliva, but the internal parts of the mound are made of material that has been worked by the termites and contains organic material.

Ruelle investigated the growth of termite mounds, which are constantly enlarging and changing in shape and form. This building behaviour has been explained (or perhaps one should say 'explained away') as a kind of vacuum activity or insatiable building drive. That it is associated with homeostasis of the nest was indicated when a mound was enclosed in a plastic tent. On each of four occasions when this was done, the termites responded within forty-eight hours by building a rash of new pinnacles on to the top of the mound. There was no vestige of such activity in mounds in the neighbouring area. The walls of these new parts were extremely porous suggesting that their function was to allow a greater quantity of air to escape from the mound. It was clear that regulation had been achieved, because immediately the dome was removed, the temperature and carbon dioxide concentration in the hive fell to unusually low levels and did not reach their normal steady state levels for a week.

The building activity takes place mainly during the rainy season, when the mound wall is kept fairly porous and wind has a relatively large effect on the nest atmosphere. After the beginning of the dry season the outer wall is thickened by the filling in of many of the superficial galleries. This compensates for the porosity which tends to increase as the wall dries out.

There is still a great deal to be learned about the behaviour of this amazingly versatile insect, *Macrotermes natalensis*. But we should perhaps now consider how other species have coped with the problem of gas exchange. Some species, such as *Microcerotermes* amd *Amitermes* have nests with thin outer walls which makes gas exchange fairly easy. Obviously there must be some compromise here, for unless, as we have seen may occur, the nest is sited in forest land where the climatic conditions are relatively stable, there will be little insulation against temperature changes. A large amount of the CO_2 produced must come from the fungus gardens; in fact it has been suggested that the main function of these is to heat and humidify the air.[108] Accordingly, it is not surprising to find that in nests of subterranean species fungus gardens, where they exist, are fairly widely dispersed, or that there is communication with the exterior, as in *Odontotermes* or *Protermes*. It is a little more difficult to suggest how *Macrotermes bellicosus* copes with the situation. The enormous mounds of this species may have walls six feet thick in which galleries are met with only rarely. However, it has been noted that the nest of this species develops underground with one enormous fungus garden surrounded by a thin clay shell (the *idiotheca*).[63] As the mound forms above ground the idiotheca disintegrates and the fungus garden is broken up to form smaller dispersed gardens. In other words it seems that the mound, when it is a closed system with no external openings, must be very large in order to support the fungus gardens. In the course of development the nest of this species is characterised by its lateral development, compared with the predominantly vertical axis of development in *M. natalensis*, and there is a tendency for division into more or less distinct units.

Finally, it must be admitted that nothing is yet known about homeostatic mechanisms in the most architecturally refined of all nests: those of *Apicotermes*. But it is hard not to believe that the pore system of the walls and the coarse sand layer around the nest are not part of the apparatus for controlling the nest climate. In fact, it is difficult not to believe that the Creator designed the nests in an inspired moment, drilled holes in the walls, and left them in the sand as homes for dispossessed termites! That this is not so has been shown, a little inappropriately perhaps, by Father Bouillon[15] who found that the nests are continually *growing*. We shall refer to this phenomenon shortly.

Nest-building behaviour

It is relatively easy to discuss the structure and functioning of a termite nest but very difficult to conceive how it was possible for the termites to build it. This is a field of biological enquiry that has scarcely been entered upon. The structures spring ultimately from the nervous systems of individuals with brains smaller than pin-heads, and those brains contain only something of the order of 10^5 nerve cells, whereas the human brain contains nearly a billion times this number. In view of this, it is difficult to entertain the idea that every termite has a concept of the completed edifice before it begins to build, and therefore it is likely that sensory mechanisms coordinating the behaviour of individuals will play an important role in the shaping of nest structure.

Anyone building a house cannot do this without a plan, and some means of interpreting the plan in terms of special measurements, and a means of coordinating the activity. Professor Grassé has made detailed observations on the building behaviour of various mound-building termites.[49,52] His general findings were that termites go through a sequence of actions, fetching and carrying particles and cementing them into place with a salivary secretion (*Cubitermes, Cephalotermes* and *Apicotermes*) or with 'mortar' of faecal origin (*Macrotermes*). This sequence is not a rigid one and a termite might change to doing something else in the middle of it. *Macrotermes* workers begin building at random, but when particles achieve a certain density on the ground they become foci for building activity with the result that pillars are formed. When the pillars attain a certain height they provide a new stimulus situation for the termites which then begin to build at right angles towards adjacent pillars so that arches are formed. Neighbouring arches are joined so that a complete roof is then formed. The presence of a queen stimulates building, and, often standing on her back to build, the *Macrotermes* workers that Grassé studied soon built an arched roof that completely covered their queen.

On the basis of his observations, Grassé proposed a new behavioural concept, *stigmergy*, to explain nest-building. The essence of this is that the material results of behaviour at each stage act as releasers for the next stage. Thus particles of a certain density on the ground release pillar building, pillars of a certain critical height (about 4–5 mm for *Cubitermes* and about 5–6 mm for *Macrotermes*) release arch building, and so on. Interestingly, this idea is one that was put forward many years ago to explain the building of nests by birds. The converse idea, that the bird has some kind of neural template in its brain and continually matches its sensory impressions of the nest with this template until it has built the 'correct' nest, has also been put forward. Not unexpectedly, perhaps, experiments have shown that neither one of these ideas provides a complete explanation. For example, even in the canary, which builds a relatively simple nest, the integration of nest-building behaviour patterns depends on a multiplicity of factors including learning, inhibitory and excitatory stimuli from the nest-cup, and changes in sensitivity of the animal's brood-patch which are in turn mediated by changes in hormone levels.[80] Evidence for a plan in the form of a template has been difficult to establish. In Weaver birds, which build a complex hanging-basket type nest, Crook[28] found that a tubular entrance added to the nest of one species which does not normally have a tube was always rapidly removed. Other species may have such a tube and do not seem to object to additions to it. This might be taken as evidence that the birds are aware of what the nest should look like.

In view of this, it might be wrong to think of stigmergy as an 'explanation', and there are indications from work on *Zootermopsis* that this concept disguises the complexity of the behaviour. If nymphs or larvae of this species are put into glass tubes with sawdust they show building behaviour patterns which are very similar to those of most termites, including the mound-builders. The sequence of behaviour can be understood with reference to

Fig. 22. Nest-building commonly begins with a phase of exploratory behaviour during which a termite stops at one point and makes repeated probing movements with its antennae (*a*). It then turns and goes downwards (*b*). The termite grasps a particle between its mandibles, and usually returns to its point of departure following an odour trail (*d*). The weight of the particle appears to be of no consequence to the insect, and termites will often struggle with very heavy particles that they cannot carry properly. There is some sort of selection of size by the mouthparts, but this operates only at one end of the particle so that its length is not assessed. It is interesting in this respect that caddis-fly larvae also take no account of weight when selecting particles for their cases, but on the other hand they do make a test of shape and fit of the particles.

When the termite returns to its original position it reverses through 180° bringing the tip of the abdomen into the place previously occupied by its head, and expels a droplet of liquid 'mortar' from the anus (*e*). It then turns again through 180°, and when the antennae touch the mortar the particle is pressed into it with a rocking movement (*f*). At intervals, the particle is released by the mandibles and held loosely between the palps. If it does not move, the termite releases it, turns, and goes downwards (*b*) guided by odour trail and gravitational stimuli. This is not the only possible sequence of building and the other main variants are shown in the figure.

Hoyle[93] suggested that the complex stereotyped behaviour of insects can be understood either as the playing of something equivalent to a neural 'tape recording' in the nervous system, or alternatively that when a piece of behaviour is under way the input from sensory receptors is compared with another sort of neural record thereby ensuring that the insect does the right things. A simple analogy to this would be represented by the problem of getting someone to type out the word 'building' on a typewriter with blank keys. You could either provide the person with a map indicating the keys in the sequence to be pressed, or alternatively, leave the person to try all the keys rapidly until they came to 'b' and then again until they came to 'u', and so on. The latter method, if it can be done quickly, less is open to error because there is a check at every stage.

There is evidence that the 'sensory tape' or comparison system is involved in the nest-building behaviour of *Zootermopsis*. For example, if a particle is dropped during (*d*), (*e*), or (*f*) the behaviour will not continue until another particle has been fetched or one nearby has been grasped. If cement is not expelled from the anus during (*e*) the termite will continue turning back and turning again until the cement is expelled. In (*f*), if the particle moves against the palps when released by the mandibles the rocking movements will be continued. This evidence suggests that each component of the behaviour has sensory feed-back mechanisms —the termite must receive specific sensory information indicating that one component is complete before another can continue. Once one component has been completed, it never occurs again in the same sequence.

From Fig. 23 there is seen to be a basic sequence *a-b-c-f-d-b*, with (*e*), the action involving deposition of mortar, interlinked at some point. This could be taken to indicate the way in which the nest-building habit evolved. It could have been through the association and compounding of two similar behaviour patterns: the removal to the exterior of particles produced by excavation of cavities in wood, and the act of defaecating outside the 'nest'. In support of this one may add that *Zootermopsis* larvae will sometimes defaecate into a fresh breach in the nest.

We now have an idea of how the basic operations of a termite engaged in nest-building may be controlled. The distinction made between plan and interpretation no longer seems a very real one. It seems that these will be explained in terms of sensory stimuli, some of which will help to co-ordinate the activities of the termites. In *Zootermopsis* some of these important sensory factors are known. This termite shows a pronounced tendency to build on upward-facing edges, and also to build where light enters. The building activity tends to be focussed where particles are already present—similar to the phenomenon Grassé observed—and this is largely because odour trails are used in building. If a termite starts building in some position it tends to return there and the odour trail it uses in orientation attracts other termites to that position. The positions at which building takes place in this insect are governed by an extreme sensitivity to air movement: there is evidence that individuals can detect air movements one thousandth the amplitude of those present in a closed room.[90] When kept in vessels in the laboratory, *Zootermopsis* will seal off points where air enters, filling in the gap between the rim and the lid of their container, and will often build platforms over the

wood in which they are living and so succeed in isolating themselves in their own airspace. This reaction is mediated by the
sensitivity to moving air, but it also ensures that humidity is
kept high in the nest. A high humidity is necessary for building
to occur, but a fall in relative humidity is unlikely to be a stimulus
to build since termites take an unusually long time to react in an
humidity gradient—up to several days, for example, in *Nasutitermes*.[41]

The hyper-sensitivity to air movement may explain a number
of other features of termite behaviour, for example the renowned
and rather unpopular ability of dry-wood termites to eat their

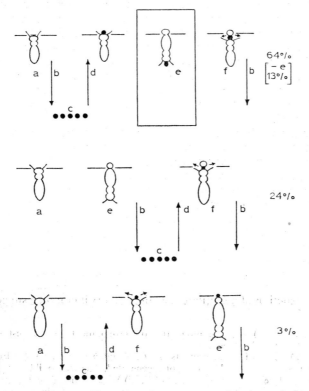

Fig. 23 Diagram illustrating the sequences of actions observed
in the building behaviour of *Zootermopsis nevadensis*. The percentage occurrences of the different patterns are given.

way through furniture leaving a paper-thin shell between themselves and the outside wall. They often, therefore, remain undetected until the whole piece suddenly collapses.

The sensitivity to air movement and the sensitivity to trail pheromones are likely to be very important factors in ordering the structure of termite nests. Pheromonal gradients are likely to centre on the queen in the middle of the nest and these could explain the existence of gradients of building material towards the centre of the nest. When they were observed building in petri dishes, *Cephalotermes* workers selected only fine-grain particles when building around the queen[49].

We have seen that a feature of many mound nests is a system of air ducts which facilitates the circulation and exchange of air. The establishment of this system could be explained in terms of reactions of the termites to air movement. Convection currents may be set up in the nest as it develops and these could provide a sort of invisibile scaffolding for the termites so that they would tend to preserve them by building around them. In this way the air currents would be encased in a shell in the peripheral regions of the nest.

Obviously, there must be an abundance of sensory factors that influence nest-building in termites, either by affecting their general motivation or by directing and coordinating their activity. Our areas of ignorance here are very large indeed. Some termites will orientate themselves with respect to magnetic fields.[9] Is this responsiveness important in the construction of the compass mounds? Or is an explanation more likely to be found in the inhibition of building in certain directions by the effects of thermal radiation? These are the sort of questions one hopes will be answered in coming years.

There have been experiments on the repair of termite nests, similar to those carried out on bird nests. Where repair or reconstruction of a mutilated portion occurs it could be suggested,

---

Fig. 24 (*a*) Possible modalities of development of the nest of *Cubitermes fungifaber*.

(*b*) Mutilation experiments on *C. fungifaber* nests. (i) A piece cut from a 'resting' nest is not regenerated. The new building that took place within 45 days is shaded. (ii) When a piece is cut from a nest in which the cap is under construction, there is limited compensation in the cap only.

(After Noirot and Noirot-Timothée[132]).

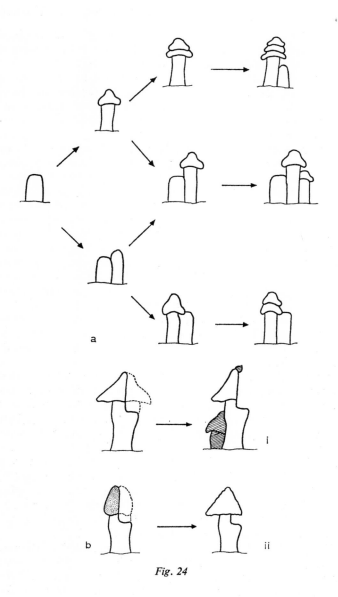

Fig. 24

again, that this shows that the animal 'knows' what the finished nest 'should look like'. Such an explanation has, in fact, been proposed to explain the behaviour of hunting wasps which will repair holes made in their brood cells. But it has been criticised on the grounds that, without knowing the sensory factors concerned, it is difficult to know whether the repair is a reaction to the discrepancy between a complete and a mutilated nest or to stimuli presented by the edges of the hole.

As might be expected from what we have learnt so far, there is no conclusive evidence for the theory which requires a concept of the completed nest form. Experiments have been done on the nests of *Cubitermes fungifaber* in the Ivory Coast.[132] Here, it seems that the termites are not quite sure how the nest should look in the first place. (Possible growth patterns are shown in Fig. 24a.) The experimenters first took the pillar of the nest and laid this horizontally on the ground. If the colony survived the operation, they either abandoned the nest and reconstructed it several metres away, or built a new nest, using the horizontal column as a base. When the colony was in the 'resting' state, during which growth of the nest does not take place, removal of part of the nest was not compensated for other than by occlusion of the opened galleries (Fig. 24b.) Only in parts of the nest which were in the process of being built was there any compensation for mutilation.

It seems that examples of the regeneration of parts of termite nests after mutilation can be explained not as attempts to remodel the nests to their original form, but as new growths which are initiated but not directed by the effects of the mutilation. Observations of Emerson and Hingston can be explained in this way. The former destroyed the lower part of a nest of *Cubitermes intercalatus* (Fig. 17) built on the trunk of a tree. After ten weeks an unattached radially symmetrical nest had been regenerated from the base of the tree by the same termite colony. Hingston[81] removed eighteen rain-shedding ridges from the tree trunk above a nest of *Constrictotermes cavifrons* (Fig. 17). At the end of six weeks eight of these ridges had been re-formed.

The problem of rebuilding the nest is presented continuously to every termite colony as it increases in size. Different species have different ways of coping with the problem. *Cubitermes* adds new pillars or new domes, and *Macrotermes natalensis* builds new towers on to its mound. *Apicotermes,* however, is clearly faced with a severe problem and it is surprising to find that the nest does increase in size. Nevertheless, Bouillon[15] has shown that this must be so. It appears to be accomplished by what one might call 'moulting backwards'. Whereas the insects themselves increase in size by forming a new cuticle under their existing one and then shedding the outer cuticle and expanding in the process, they increase the size of their nests by resorbing the existing wall and building a new one outside it. It took clever detective work to establish this: apart from the difficulty of observing the process because the nests are underground, it is very rare to find one in the process of reconstruction. Bouillon suggests that reconstruction must take place very rapidly because the colony is then very vulnerable to attack.

E

7

CONCEPTS OF THE SOCIAL BEHAVIOUR

OF INSECTS

In a recent discussion on science and literature, Sir Peter Meda-war[123] maintains that all advance in scientific understanding begins with an imaginative conception of what might be true. 'It is the invention of a Possible World, or of a tiny fraction of that world.' When applied to the study of social insects, this statement is immensely illuminating. The behaviour of termites and other social insects is astonishing to us because of its many facets and apparent complexity. Phenomena promoting cohesion of a colony and cooperation among individuals have allowed an exploitation of new possibilities in behaviour that are not seen in non-social insects. Especially, the striking examples of con-certed behaviour that many people have observed have led them to see aspects of their own behaviour reflected in the activities of the insects, and have been, consequently, happy to conclude that social insects are intelligent. 'Ants', said Sir John Lubbock[106] over eighty years ago, 'have a fair claim to rank next to man in the scale of intelligence.' His contemporary, Romanes,[139] explained the way of thought of many early scientists: 'Starting from what I know subjectively of the operations of my own individual mind, and the activities which in my own organisms they prompt, I pro-ceed by analogy to infer from the observable activities of other organisms what are the mental operations that underlie them.'

So the first theory of termite behaviour was an analogy, an invented possible world, which embodies a kind of narcissism that dies hard among many people even today—as the corre-spondence columns of newspapers show from time to time. The idea that the insect society is a kingdom with the various classes of individuals going intelligently about their work would be laughed out of any court of biologists today, and it seems amazing that brilliant men should have thought in these terms so recently. Because the process is very slow, we tend to be unaware of the way in which scientific discoveries continually reshape our ideas, acting like a sieve with the meshes becoming finer and finer, so that the larger and less accurately formed analogies have increasing difficulty in getting through. Nevertheless, the suggestion that invisible substances called pheromones are to be found floating around in the colony and that these influence the behaviour of the individuals would doubtless have seemed obscurantist to the Victorian scientists. We should also remember that the 'data' with which they worked were mostly anecdotes in which it was easy to see repeated examples of 'problems' being 'solved', 'purpose' in behaviour, 'reasoned' action, and so forth. Examples where these interpretations were not possible never became anecdotes!

The superorganism

For many people, another analogy subsequently became more acceptable, and this was the *Superorganism* theory, in which the colony was considered as a complete organism. In an essay published in 1911, Wheeler,[165] a great expert on social insects, drew the parallel between an ant colony and some kind of gigantic protozoan. The queen ant was said to be equivalent to the nucleus of the cell, the mass of ants to the plasmodium (main body), and the files of foraging ants to the pseudopodial extensions used in feeding.

After the First World War, books were published by two naturalist-philosophers, Maeterlinck[118] and Marais,[119] who put forward the superorganism theory independently, and made great play of the 'group soul' of the colony.

Maeterlinck had his metaphors rather mixed, for while he believed that the insect colony was a composite organism he was preoccupied with comparisons with human society. In *The Life of the White Ant* he wrote: 'In the termitary the gods of communism have become insatiable molochs . . . the species which appears to be the most highly civilised also appears to be the most enslaved and the most pitiable.' Termites, he asserted, also possess a soul or 'occult power which governs'. Associated with this soul was a 'memory' that accounted for the behaviour patterns and instincts of the species which had been assimilated during the millions of years of evolution of the composite organism.

Eugene Marais, a South African, who is also known for his field studies on the behaviour of baboons, developed, in some detail, a superorganism theory in his book *The Soul of the White Ant*. He believed implicitly that the termitary really was an individual organism, and expected natural selection one day to produce a termitary capable of locomotion so that it could transport itself across the veldt. Some of the equivalences he made were between the wall of the mound and the skin, the fungus gardens and the stomach and liver, the workers and soldiers and red and white blood cells, the queen cell and the skull, the queen and the brain, and the king and the male sex organ.

The American zoologist A. E. Emerson[37] has tailored the superorganism theory (or *Supra*organism as he prefers to call it) to fit more easily with biological facts that were unknown to his romantic predecessors. Emerson suggests that, for example, transmission of excitability among the insects parallels the activity of the nervous system; that the control of caste development is similar to the control of tissue differentiation by hormones; and that the colony odour results in an antagonism between individuals of different colonies which is like immunological reactions between host and foreign tissues.

The superorganism theory does not, of course, deserve its name, because it is an analogy, like the 'kingdom' concept. Both begin with a conceptual framework into which the facts are fitted as they accumulate. Their *raison d'être* lies in the framework being one that is easily understood and retained, and their value is that they provide us with a language to use in talking about insect societies. The dangers are that facts which do not fit very well are twisted or excluded. Every analogy obviously becomes meaningless if pushed too far, otherwise the two things would be indistinguishable, but this does not mean that the exercise is wasted—far from it. Bondi[14] has pointed out that although the earth has been proved quite convincingly to be round, architects since the beginning of civilisation have proceeded on the assumption that it is flat. This is quite the best approximation for people building houses. Similarly, the idea that cellular and caste differentiation proceed on similar lines is a good one for the experimental biologist, but the suggestion that a constant temperature is maintained in the termite mound in the same way as it is maintained in the human body is plain nonsense.

The principal use that Emerson has made of the superorganism theory is in the analysis of evolutionary trends in termites. If the colony is regarded as a unit, it is possible to talk about its adaptations to a way of life in the same way that one talks about the adaptations of a single animal. For example, nest structure has to be regarded as the equivalent of body form and has been used to separate species of *Apicotermes* that were almost indistinguishable in other ways. Again, it has been possible to see evolutionary trends towards increased homeostasis in termite nests, which helps in solving taxonomic problems.

In these respects, then, the view of the colony as a superorganism has been fruitful. As Schiller said of knowledge, 'To one she is the high and heavenly goddess, to the other, a diligent cow that provides him with milk.' Equally, it has to be recognised that an analogy provides practical hypotheses and stimulates scientific research only for some people. For others with different interests it is apt to be an alluring concept that it is difficult to resist.

Biologists and psychologists who were interested in the general aspects of animal behaviour naturally tended to overlook the superorganism theory, which had little relevance to them. In the early part of the century, there were many who were primarily interested in learning in animals. Animals that could not learn new tricks like running mazes or pressing levers were politely ignored and their behaviour was labelled with terms like 'reflex' and 'instinct'. This led to a dichotomy between the concepts of instinct and learning which exists to the present day in the writings of some biologists, and has its roots in the bold and provocative assertions of the seventeenth-century philosopher, Descartes, who maintained that animals were automata and that their behaviour was little more than the running down of clockwork.

Reflex and instinct

Sir Charles Sherrington, the great English physiologist, investigated the nervous mechanisms of behaviour in vertebrate animals using 'spinal' animals in which the spinal cord was severed to eliminate the effect of the brain on the trunk and limbs. Various pieces of behaviour could be elicited from these animals, such as scratching movements, postural adjustments, and even locomotion in a limited sense. The behaviour was thus far from simple, although without the controlling action of the brain it was fairly stereotyped. Sherrington explored the laws of the simplest of these reflexes, and although he emphasised that a 'simple reflex', disconnected (as it were) from the rest of the nervous system was an abstract concept, use of this term proved to be a tactical error. Many biologists came to think of animals, and insects in particular, as 'bundles of reflexes' acting on a sort of telephone-exchange principle, where applying a particular stimulus was like dialling a number which produced an invariable automatic response.

This, as Professor J. S. Kennedy[99] has argued with great cogency, was a travesty of Sherrington's ideas, but one person who reacted against it was Konrad Lorenz, soon to be known as the founder of ethology, defined as the scientific study of animal behaviour. He had a passionate interest in animals of all kinds and used great patience in observing their behaviour. He realised behaviour was too adaptable and variable in threshold to be understood in terms of 'simple reflexes' and suggested instead that it comprised instinctive activities which were different from reflexes because each was associated with a kind of nervous energy, and fluctuations in this energy accounted for the variability of behaviour.

Instincts were thus understood as essentially stereotyped behaviour patterns that were genetically inherited like bodily features. Tinbergen helped in the formulation of what have come to be known as 'ethological' theories. He emphasised the hierarchical organisation of instinctive behaviour.

To understand some of the ethological concepts, let us take the example of the courtship behaviour of the Grayling butterfly. This is a brown butterfly that is common on heathlands in southern England. When the males are sexually mature, they are affected by a reproductive *drive* which causes them to take up positions on the ground. This introductory phase of the instinct is called *appetitive behaviour*, and it is very variable in content. If a female flies past, she provides a *releasing* stimulus to the male, who flies up and chases her. If she is responsive, she alights, and the appetitive behaviour terminates with various ritual movements of the antennae and wings. Mating, the *consummatory act,* follows, which results in the release of nervous 'energy' associated with this instinct, which will not be further activated until the 'energy' has had time to build up again. One can also see hierarchical organisation in this behaviour, since actions start by being rather general, but become more and more specific.

It will at once be evident that this theory of behaviour has similarities with others we have examined. It provides us with a new terminology and a new framework on which the facts can be arranged. The essential 'invention' is that nervous energy, or rather of specific energies, each associated with a particular instinct or drive, and the possibility of *describing* behaviour in terms of being damned up, and flowing this way and that has been an enormous stimulus to research, especially on the behaviour of animals in the field. But once again, there are realms in this analogy—for that is essentially what it is—where it is not useful and even where it is downright misleading.

It is difficult to describe flight and colony foundation in termites in ethological terms, and even then not illuminating. Plainly, the actual emergence and flight as well as the tandem are appetitive behaviour, but is the building of the first cell equivalent to the consummatory act? Or the act of copulation? Or the loss of wings, because full appetitive behaviour cannot be repeated after that? Does the reproductive drive begin at emergence, or when the long-winged nymphs are produced? Clearly, these questions are not going to enhance our understanding of why things happen when they do in termites.

Likewise, while a description of nest-building behaviour in ethological terms is vaguely possible, it is simply not useful. Who can define the consummatory act there? Grassé's concept of stigmergy is more useful, because in the framework of this it is possible to define the various steps in the process of construction and to focus attention on the processes of social integration. Unfortunately, descriptions and definitions are very apt to appear as explanations and this is true both of stigmergy, and the ethology of Lorenz and Tinbergen.

Kennedy[99] has labelled theories such as these *psychological*. This is no disparagement. The psychologist needs to talk about behaviour and the various factors that influence it in a way that short-cuts physiology, because otherwise it would take him a great deal longer to say anything. The real danger, as both Kennedy and Medawar agree, occurs when these short-cuts become such universal currency that no one thinks about the physiological problems. A child may, after all, be an imbecile because it cannot metabolise a substance called phenylanaline, but the supporters of Freud's 'possible world' would have found an explanation in terms of the subconscious. Kennedy argues, with particular reference to insect behaviour, that more attention should be directed towards a study of the physiological mechanisms. Perhaps the most important feature, which we take for granted, is that an animal can do only one thing at a time. This means that all the other behaviour patterns are inhibited, which in turn implies a great complexity of interconnection within the nervous system that both inhibit and excite. Consequently, it is scarcely surprising that different individuals may vary considerably in their readiness to do things, and one does not need to invoke different levels of behavioural energy to explain this. Kennedy, in fact, has been able to show how the behaviour of aphids can be understood in the simple physiological terms that Sherrington used to describe as reflexes.

Approach/withdrawal theory

T. C. Schneirla[149,150], the American biologist, has been a strong critic of the European ethologists. In proposing his Approach/ withdrawal theory he has thrown the term 'instinct' overboard, pointing out that, especially in the very young animal, the environment exerts a continual effect on the development of behaviour patterns. So the idea that instincts can be split off, as it were, from the rest of the behaviour of the animal because they are stereotyped, and *therefore* that they are genetically determined, is fundamentally unsound. Schneirla maintains that at the roots of the behaviour of all animals are the actions of approach to low-intensity stimuli and withdrawal from high-intensity stimuli. The development of these in the very young animal is a complex process, in which the maturing behaviour patterns may be continuously modified by the effects of environmental stimuli, but these formative processes mould the stems from which the more intricate patterns of adult animals eventually blossom.

Schneirla was led to his theory through studies of the social behaviour of the driver ant, *Eciton hamatum*. This species lives a nomadic life, ranging over large areas of country. The truly nomadic phase of their behaviour, however, in which foraging takes place over large areas using extensive pheromone trails, lasts only about seventeen days at a time. The insects form a bivouac in the evenings, which consists of a tent formed of their own bodies, sheltering their nest-mates underneath. The nomadic phase alternates with a 'statary' phase in which the ants stay put for about twenty days and have few raiding parties. Schneirla found that this cycle of behaviour was related to the reproductive activity of the queen. This was in turn determined by the amount of trophallaxis that occurred between her and the workers. When the brood is developing, the queen gets relatively little attention in the form of trophallaxis, and this suppresses her egg-laying, but when the brood approaches maturity her share of attention increases, which stimulates her to lay.

Here, then, is a cycle of activity that is stereotyped, but ultimately dependent on trophallactic activity. Trophallaxis, Schneirla believes, is a behaviour pattern that may arise through simple conditioning processes in the newly hatched insect. Reactions of turning towards sources of weak stimulation presented by the nest-mates in the form of colony odour or slow movements will tend to be rewarded by food and thereby strengthened.

Approach/withdrawal theory does not suppose that termites learn to build nests: that would be inconceivable, but it is conceivable that the young termites must develop in the society of the nest in order for normal reactions to their nest-mates to be formed. It is these that are responsible for coordinated activities that are the outstanding features of insect societies, and that have been described by Grassé and his co-workers under terms like *effet de groupe,* and *effet de masse,* which are essentially 'psychological'. Many aspects of these phenomena will almost certainly be explained in terms of pheromones. The presence of the queen provides an essential stimulus to the building activity of disturbed *Macrotermes* workers, and they will build around her in light and open air. A similar phenomenon suggestive of pheromone production by the queen is seen in honeybees.[29] Fifty bees will build in the presence of a live queen, but 200 are needed in the presence of a dead one, and 10,000 are required if there is no queen present. It is known that trail pheromones play a part in building in *Zootermopsis,* and it is known that in the mounds of some species there is a gradient of materials focussing on the queen cell, for which the finest particles are selected. There is a rich field of research here, in the effects that pheromones may have in modifying cooperative activities in termites.

Nervous mechanisms of behaviour

The arguments of Kennedy and Schneirla lead us compellingly to the conclusion that objective or physiological terms must be used in the investigation of mechanisms of animal behaviour.

The concepts that have been used, especially in the study of social insects, are frameworks on which to arrange our knowledge, but in *some* respects they are all tendentious. In Kennedy's view, psychological concepts still short-circuit our thinking, and thus replace physiological analysis. 'The issue here is not the meaning of words but the conduct of research.' With this in mind, let us re-examine two facets of termite behaviour, which both involve sequences of actions: nest-building and swarming.

In the nest-building of *Zootermopsis* there is one particular sequence of actions that predominates, but other sequences are possible and do occur. Why should this be so? To explain this, we can imagine that each action has its own separate nervous mechanism and that when this has run down it will stimulate the next one down the line, and so on. But we must not forget that to perform each action correctly the termite must receive a feed-back of information about its position and posture from instant to instant. This suggests an alternative explanation: does this information, as Grassé believes, select the next action? It seems not, for *Zootermopsis* usually produces every element in the sequence, even if this means depositing cement on top of a particle that the insect has just fixed firmly into place. Further, no action is repeated in the same sequence, and the next action will not follow unless the preceding one has been completed. This supports the idea of interlinked nervous mechanisms, but the sequence can also be changed by altering the stimulus situation: a greater degree of exposure to moving air will result in relatively more of the sequencies in the second line of Fig. 23 and less of those in the first line.

It is therefore possible to envisage that the behaviour is under the control of central nervous mechanisms in which the sequence is roughly set and that fine control of the sequence and the orientation of individual actions is achieved by sensory information. Hoyle's concepts of sensory and motor tapes are relevant in this connection and have already been discussed.

The predation on termite swarms is very high, and therefore it is not surprising to see behavioural adaptations in many species that make pairing and colony foundation a more certain process. In termites such as *Kalotermes flavicollis* the shedding of wings may take some minutes and the tandem is not very secure. It may consist of individuals of either sex following the other, or even of two individuals of the same sex, and may last up to two days. *Pseudacanthotermes spiniger*, on the other hand, is much more efficient. The wings are shed instantaneously, the tandem lasts two to ten minutes, and the male always follows the female. In *Anoplotermes* the tandem is a stage further towards forcible abduction; the male hangs on to the female with its mandibles.

Again there is some evidence that the sequence of events is ordered by sensory stimuli. For example, wing shedding occurs on settling and tandem behaviour starts after the female has extruded a scent gland. However, in some species there is evidence that one action is invariably a prerequisite for the next. A certain period of flight may be necessary before tandem behaviour can occur.

Behaviour sequences in courtship have been investigated in various insects, and there are some similarities to be seen with sequences in termite behaviour. The courtship of the male fruit fly, *Drosophila melanogaster,* consists of three elements, *orientation, vibration* of the wings, and *licking* of the female.[7] These, however, do not occur in any fixed order, neither does the sequence appear to be determined by stimuli from the female. It seems that the mechanisms here are not interlinked, but that they are all activated together. A fundamentally different example is provided by the mating behaviour of the cockroach *Byrsotria fumigata.*[6] The male performs a sequence of about seven actions in alternation with seven of the female, so that the chain largely depends on the reaction of the one releasing the next action of the other. This starts with the production of a pheromone by the female which releases an alert posture in the male, which then walks towards her and touches her with his antennae. If she is receptive, she adopts an alert posture which then releases 'wing pumping' in the male when he perceives the pheromone by direct contact of his antennae with her body. Now occasionally, the first production of the pheromone by the female will release both antennal waving and wing pumping. Likewise perception of the pheromone by contact will release wing pumping and the next item in the male display, which is wing raising and turning.

It appears, therefore, that behaviour sequences in insects can vary from an assortment of actions which are unconnected except in the sense that they are all responses to more or less the same stimuli, to sequences that are determined largely by changes that affect the sense organs of the insect, and to sequences which are controlled by sensory input but 'hardened' by apparent links in the central nervous system.

It is not hard to accept the idea that this is also an evolutionary succession, i.e. that in courtship behaviour or nest-building behaviour natural selection has favoured in some insects processes that make the sequence more precise. A concomitant of this has been that behaviour has become more stereotyped in this respect. Instead of the insect being like a key board, where each stimulus is a key that releases a particular reaction independently of others, the keys have been loosely linked in some way so that it is much easier to play one after another has been played. This makes it easier for the pianist who can play longer and more attractive tunes without making mistakes.

The idea of interlinked mechanisms in the central nervous systems is also an 'invention'; these mechanisms may or may not exist, but the concept provides a stimulus to neurophysiologists and behaviourists to try to find them. If they prove not to be there, the exercise will still have been a useful one because we will have learnt a lot of the nervous system in the looking. This brings us to a consideration of the insect brain itself. Where might these 'mechanisms' lie? What functions do the various parts of the brain perform? The answers to these questions are known, at least broadly, for the vertebrate brain, but when we come to the insect brain the extent of our ignorance is vast.

A great deal of what we know about the insect brain has come from studies on social insects. The brain of *Zootermopsis angusicollis* contains something of the order of 10^5 nerve cells. As in other insects, these have many long branches which intertwine in a seemingly disorganised fashion in large portions of the brain. In some regions they are associated together in a more organised manner to form compact and easily recognisable structures. Among the most important of these are the *mushroom bodies* (corpora pedunculata) and the *central body*, which are evident in the section in Fig. 23.

The mushroom bodies were discovered in ants over a hundred years ago by Dujardin, who considered them to be the seat of intelligence in insects. A later study by von Alten[2] supported this idea by showing that these structures progressed in size and complexity from the rather simple Hymenoptera, such as sawflies, to the social bees and wasps. Thus in sawflies, the cap or calyx of the mushroom is a simple club-shaped body; in gall wasps it is saucer-shaped; in parastic wasps, which often show a quite complicated pattern of searching behaviour for their hosts, it is cup-shaped; and in the social bees and wasps it is in the shape of a deep beaker (Fig. 23). Along with the increase in surface area of the calyx, the relative thickness of the stalk also increases. In honeybees, social wasps and hornets, the calyces are extremely striking and each of the four cups is two-layered. The relative size of the mushroom bodies differs among the castes; the workers have the largest (13·5% of the brain tissue), the queens the next largest (9·2%), and the drones the smallest (5·6%). A similar relationship is found in ants, where they are largest in workers and smallest in males.

The role of the mushroom bodies in the behaviour of crickets and grasshoppers has been investigated by Professor Huber[94] of Tübingen. The technique he used was to insert very fine wire electrodes into the brains of these insects, and he was able to make the insects sing their different songs if particular parts of the stalk complex of the mushroom bodies were stimulated electrically. Stimulation of areas in the calyces actually stopped the songs in mid-course. Destroying other areas in the stalks resulted in the insect singing until it was exhausted, and quite a-typical songs were produced by stimulating the central body. As a result of these and other experiments, Huber concluded that the calyces are foci for information from the sense organs. On the basis of the information, they determine whether or not singing occurs and the nature and duration of the song. These decisions are then sent along to the central body which translates them into particular patterns of neural activity that determine the movements of the legs (or wings) of the insect and therefore its song pattern. The mushroom bodies, therefore, are seen as association centres, with inhibitory and excitatory domains, where the information from the sense organs accumulates and is evaluated.

This view of the function of the mushroom bodies provides an explanation for their marked elaboration in social insects. We should expect to find that the mushroom bodies of termites are also well-developed, especially in those which build complex nests. Recent studies Dr Williams and I have made on this have had some surprising results. We expected to see a progression in the size of the mushroom bodies related with the complexity of the nests the insects build, but to our surprise the differences among species proved to be quite small. The cups in *Zootermopsis* are poorly developed (Fig. 25), although the stems and the branches that arise from them are very thick. But in *Macrotermes natalensis* and *Apicotermes occultus* only very simple cups are present, comparable in size with those in the dry-wood termite, *Neotermes jouteli,* and the so-called primitive termite *Mastotermes darwiniensis.* Certainly, they never attain anything like the form

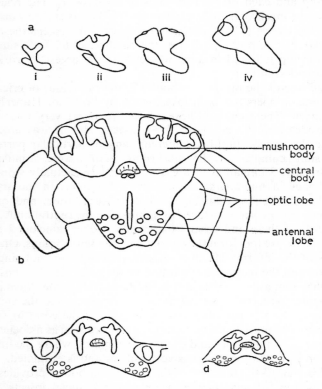

Fig. 25 (*a*) Diagram to show the relative development of mushroom bodies in hymenopteran brains: (i), sawfly; (ii), wood-wasp; (iii), parasitic wasp; (iv) social bee.

(*b*) Section through the brain of a worker wasp, (*c*) section through *Zootermopsis angusticollis* brain, (*d*) section through *Macrotermes natalensis* worker brain.

. (*a*) after von Alten[2], (*b*), (*c*) and (*d*) from Howse and Williams (unpublished). (*b*), (*c*) and (*d*) are drawn to scale, and the nerve cell bodies are only slightly smaller in the termites.

they attain in the bees and wasps. An additional and even more surprising finding is that the number of nerve cell bodies associated with the calyces is far lower in *Macrotermes* and *Apicotermes* than in the far more 'primitive' *Zootermopsis* and *Neotermes*.

There seems to be only one logical explanation for these findings, which stems from the fact that all the termites are blind, or nearly so. In the hymenopteran series, the reliance on the visual senses in behaviour gradually increases: an increase paralleled by the development of the calyces. Social bees and wasps are able to memorise features of their surroundings, and use these in orientation. This ability tends not to impress us, because it is one of which we are all easily capable and tend to take for granted, but it is a monumental achievement for the microscopical piece of tissue that we call the insect brain. The memory system demands the formation of a map somewhere within the brain, and this map might even need to be three dimensional. The massive calyces in the wasp brain, with their double-layered structure, could well be the appropriate apparatus.

This still leaves us with a paradox as far as termites are concerned. How can more complex behaviour be produced by a brain which apparently has fewer nerve cells? It is clear that an answer to this question can come only from a detailed understanding of the behaviour of the insects along with a study of their neuroanatomy and physiology. So at the end of this trail of 'possible worlds' there are new and tantalising problems for the experimental biologist.

REFERENCES

A complete bibliography of termites up to 1965 is provided by Snyder (see below). The following list relates only to works that have been referred to in the text. Review articles and the more comprehensive books are marked with an asterisk.

1. ALIBERT, J. (1963) *Insectes soc.* **10**: 1–12. (trophallaxis in *Cubitermes*)

2. ALTEN, H. v. (1910) *Jena, Z. Naturw.* **46**: 511–590. (Structure of hymenopteran brains)

3. ANDREWS, E. A. (1911) *J. Anim. Behav.* **1**: 193–228. (Behaviour of Jamaican termites)

4. ANDREWS, E. A., and MIDDLETON, A. R. (1911) *Circ. Johns Hopkins Univ.* **2**: 26–34. (Circadian activity of nasutes)

5. BANKS, N., SNYDER, T. E. (1920) *Bull. U.S. natn. Mus.* **108**: 1–228. (Biology and distribution of nearctic termites)

6. BARTH, R. H. (1964) *Behaviour* **23**: 1–30. (Mating behaviour in cockroaches)

7. BASTOCK, M., MANNING, A. (1955) *Behaviour* **8**: 85–111. (Courtship of *Drosophila*)

8. BATES, H. W. (1864) *A naturalist on the river Amazon.* London

9. BECKER, G. (1963) *Naturwissenschaften* **12**: 455. (Orientation of termites in magnetic field)

10. BECKER, G., PETROWITZ, H. J., (1967) *Naturwissenschaften* **54**: 16. (Trail pheromones)

11. BODOT, P., (1961) *C.r. hebd. Scéanc. Acad. Sci., Paris* **253**: 3053–3054. (Destruction of mounds by an ant)

12. BODOT, P. (1967) *Insectes soc.* **14**: 359–388. (Seasonal activity cycles of termites in savanna)

13. BODOT, P. (1967) *Insectes Soc.* **14**: 351–358. (Flight and colony foundation in *Allodontotermes*)

14. BONDI, H. (1967) *Assumption and Myth in Physical Theory.* Cambridge

15. BOUILLON, A. (1964) In *Études sur les Termites Africains.* Leopoldville (UNESCO) (Several papers)

16. BOUILLON, A. (1958) *Naturalistes Belges* **39**: 198–207. (Termites of Katanga)

17. BREADY, J. K., FRIEDMAN, S. (1963) *J. Insect Physiol.* **9**: 337–348. (Oxygen poisoning in *Reticulitermes*)

18. BUCHLI, H. (1956) *Insectes soc.* **3**: 131–143. (Neoteny in *Reticulitermes*)

19. BUGNION, E. (1913) *Bull. Soc. ent. Suisse* **12**: 125–139. (Sounds made by termites)

20. BUGNION, E. (1927) *Psyche Monographs No.* **1**: 1–44. (Ants and termites in Ceylon)

21. BUSNEL, R.-G. (1956) *Insectes soc.* **3**: 11–16. (Acoustic behaviour of Orthoptera)

22. BUTLER, C. G. (1967) *Biol. Rev.* **42**: 42–87. (Insect pheromones)

23. BUXTON, P. A. (1923) *Entomologist* **56**: 271–273. (Coordinated tapping in insects)

24. CASTLE, G. B. (1934) In *Termites and Termite Control.* Berkeley. (Caste determination in *Zootermopsis*)

25. CLEVELAND, L. R., HALL, S. R., SANDERS, E. P., COLLIER, J. (1934) *Mem. amer. Acad. Arts, Sci.* **17**: 185–342. (Biology and symbiosis of *Cryptocercus*)

26. COATON, W. G. H. (1947) *J. ent. Soc. sth. Afr.* **9**: 130–177. (Biology of South African wood-eating termites)

27. COATON, W. G. H. (1958) *Un. S. Afr. Dept. Agr. Sc. Bull.* **375**: 1–112. (Hodotermotid harvester termites)

28. CROOK, J. H. (1964) *Proc. zool. Soc. Lond.* **142**: 217–255. (Nest building of weaver birds)

29. DARCHEN, R. (1957) *Insectes soc.* **4**: 321–325. (Comb-building in honeybees)

30. DE BONT, A. F. (1964) In *Études sur les Termites Africains,* Ed. Bouillon. Leopoldville (UNESCO). (Termites and birds)

31. DELIGNE, J. (1965) *C. r. 5th int. Congr. Insectes Soc. Toulouse:* 131–142 (Functioning of soldier mandibles)

32. DE PLOEY, J. (1964) In *Études sur les Termites Africains,* Ed. Bouillon. Leopoldville (UNESCO). (Formation of soils in the Congo)

33. DESNEUX, J. (1956) *Revue Zool. Bot. afr.* 53: 92–97. (Nest of *Apicotermes rimulifex*)

34. DROPKIN, V. H. (1946) *J. Parasit.* 32: 247–251. (Mixing of termite colonies)

35. EMERSON, A. E. (1929) *Trans. 4th int. ent. Congr., Ithaca* 2: 722–727. (Communication among termites)

36. EMERSON, A. E. (1951) *Inst. Rech. sci. afr. centr.* 2: 149–160. (Termites in the Congo)

37. EMERSON, A. E. (1952) In *Structure et Physiologie des sociétés animales.* Paris (CNRS): 333–354. (Supraorganism concept)

38. EMERSON, A. E. (1956) *Am. Mus. Novit., No.* 1771, 1–31. (Termite taxonomy and behaviour)

39. EMERSON, A. E. (1956) *Ecology* 37: 248–258. (Climate and rebuilding of termite nests)

40. EMERSON, A. E. (1961) *Evolution, Lancaster, Pa.* 15: 115–131. (Evolution of termites)

41. ERNST, E. (1957) *Acta Tropica* 14: 97–156. (Effect of humidity on longevity and behaviour of termites)

42. ERNST, E. (1959) *Revue suisse Zool.* 66: 289–295. (Behaviour of nasute soldiers)

43.* ESCHERICH, K. (1909) *Die Termiten oder weissen Ameisen.* Leipzig

44.* ESCHERICH, K. (1911) *Termitenleben auf Ceylon.* Jena.

45. FYFE, R. V., GAY, E. J. (1938) *Aust. C. sci. ind. Res.* Pamphlet 82: 1–22. (Humidity and moisture contents of *Nasutitermes* mounds)

46.* GOETSCH, W. (1953) *Vergleichende Biologie der Insektenstaat.* Leipzig

47. GONÇALVES, C. R. SILVA, A. G. A. (1962) *Arq. Mus. Nac. Rio de Jan.* 52: 193–208. (Observations on Brazilian termites)

48. GOODALL, J. v. LAWICK, (1968) *Anim. Behav. monogr.* 1: 161–311. (Behaviour of free-living chimpanzees)

49. GRASSÉ, P.-P. (1939) *J. Psychol.* 391–396. (Reconstruction of nests by Termitidae)

50.* GRASSÉ, P.-P. (1949) In *Traité de Zoologie, Insectes* 9: Paris. (Review of the order Isoptera)

51. GRASSÉ, P.-P. (1958) *Insectes soc.* 5: 189–200. (*Cornitermes* nest)

52. GRASSÉ, P.-P. (1959) *Insectes soc.* **6**: 41–83. (Nest reconstruction, theory of stigmergy)

53. GRASSÉ, P. P., NOIROT, C. (1947) *C. r. hebd. Séanc. Acad. Sci.* **224**: 219–221. (Pseudergates of *Kalotermes*)

54 GRASSÉ, P.-P., NOIROT, C. (1948) *C. r. hebd. Séanc. Acad. Sci.* **227**: 869–871. (Humidification of nests)

55. GRASSÉ, P.-P., NOIROT, C. (1949) *Annls Sci. nat.* (*Zool.*) **10**: 149–166. (Nest and biology of *Sphaerotermes*)

56. GRASSÉ, P.-P., NOIROT, C., CLEMENT, G., BUCHLI, H. (1950) *C. r. hebd. Séanc. Acad. Sci., Paris* **230**: 892–895. (Significance of worker caste in termites)

57. GRASSÉ, P.-P., NOIROT, C. (1951) *Behaviour* **3**: 146–166. (New colonies founded by sociotomy)

58. GRASSÉ, P.-P., and NOIROT, C. (1951) *L'Année Psychol.* **50**: 273–280. (Building of foraging trails)

59. GRASSÉ, P.-P., NOIROT, C. (1951) *Annls Sci. nat.* (*Zool.*) **13**: 291–342. (Biology of Macrotermitinae)

60. GRASSÉ, P.-P., NOIROT, C. (1958) *C. r. hebd. Séanc. Acad. Sci., Paris* **246**: 1789–1795. (Life history of *Kalotermes flavicollis*)

61. GRASSÉ, P.-P., NOIROT, C. (1958) *Annls Sci. nat.* (*Zool.*) **20**: 1–28. (Air movement and nests)

62. GRASSÉ, P.-P., NOIROT, C. (1959) *Experientia* **15**: 365–372. (Evolution of symbiosis in termites)

63. GRASSÉ, P.-P., NOIROT, C. (1961) *Insectes soc.* **8**: 312–359. (Behaviour and systematics of *Macrotermes*)

64. GRASSÉ, B., SANDIAS, A. (1897) *Q. Jl. Microsc. Sci.* **39**:2 45–322; **40**: 1–82. (Biology of societies of Italian termites)

65. GREAVES, T. (1959) *Aust. Forestry* **23**: 114–120. (Termites in Australian forests)

66. GREAVES, T. (1962) *Aust. J. Zool.* **10**: 630–651. (Foraging galleries of *Coptotermes*)

67. GREAVES, T. (1964) *Aust. J. Zool.* **12**: 250–262. (Temperatures in *Coptotermes* nests)

68. GREAVES, T. (1967) *CSIRO. Divn. of Entomology Technical Paper no. 7*, Melbourne: 19–33. (*Coptotermes* colonies in tree trunks)

69. GUNTHER, J. (1953) *Inside Africa*, New York. (Termites in folklore)

70.* HAGEN, H. (1860) *Linnean Entomologica, Stettin* **10**: 12, 14. (Monographie der Termiten)

71. HARMS, J. W. (1927) *Zool. Anz.* **74**: 221–236. (Swarming of *Macrotermes gilvus*)

72.* HARRIS, W. V. (1961) *Termites, their recognition and control.* London

73. HARRIS, W. V. (1965) *Pest Articles news Summ.* (*A*) **11**: 33–43. (Termite damage and control)

74. HARRIS, W. V. (1966) *Insectes soc.* **13**: 255–266. (Termites and tropical forestry)

75. HARRIS, W. V., SANDS, W. A. (1965) *Symp. zool. Soc. Lond.* **14**: 113–131. (Social organisation of termite colonies—review)

76. HEGH, E. (1922) *Les Termites, Partie générale.* Brussels

77. HERFS, A. (1951) *Z. angew. Ent.* **33**: 69–77. (Swarming of *Reticulitermes lucifugus*)

78. HILL, G. F. (1925) *Proc. R. Soc. Vict.* **37**: 119–124. (Habits of *Mastotermes darwiniensis*)

79. HILL, G. F. (1942) *Termites* (*Isoptera*) *of the Australian region.* Melbourne

80. HINDE, R. A. (1958) *Proc. zool. Soc. Lond.* **131**: 1–48. (Nest-building behaviour of canaries)

81. HINGSTON, R. W. G. (1932) *A Naturalist in the Guiana Forest.* London

82. HOLDAWAY, F. G., GAY, F. J. (1948) *Aust. J. sci. Res. Ser. B.* **1**: 464–493. (Mound temperatures of *Nasutitermes*)

83. HÖLLDOBLER, B., MASCHWITZ, U. (1965) *Z. vergl. Physiol.* **50**: 551–568. (Swarming of red ants)

84. HOLMGREN, N. (1910–1912) *K. svenska Vetensk Akad. Handl.* 46–8. (Systematics and biology of termites)

85. HOWSE, P. E. (1962) *Symposia Genetica et biol. it.* **9**: 256–268. (Oscillatory movements of termites)

86. HOWSE, P. E. (1964) *Anim. Behav.* **12**: 284–300. (Communication by tapping in *Zootermopsis*)

87. HOWSE, P. E. (1964) *J. Insect Physiol.* **10**: 409–424. (Physiology of termite subgenual organ)

88. HOWSE, P. E. (1965) *Insectes soc.* **12**: 335–346. (Communication by oscillatory movements)

89. HOWSE, P. E. (1965) *Proc. R. ent. Soc. Lond.* (*A*) **40**: 137–146. (Structure of sense organs of *Zootermopsis*)

90. HOWSE, P. E. (1966) *Nature, Lond.* **210**: 967–968. (Air movement and termite behaviour)

91. HOWSE, P. E. (1968) *Insectes soc.* **15**: 54–50. (Division of labour in *Zootermopsis*)

92. HOWSE, P. E. (1968) *Symp. zool. Soc. Lond.* **23**: 167–198. (Fine structure of chordotonal organs)

93. HOYLE, G. (1964) In *Neural Theory and Modelling*, Ed. Reiss-Stanford

94. HUBER, F. (1960) *Z. vergl. Physiol.* **44**: 60–132. (Function of insect brain)

95. HUMMEL, H. (1968) *Beiträge zur Kenntnis der Pheromone*, Marburg/Lahn. (Inaugural dissertation)

96. KAISER, P. (1954) *Zool. Anz.* **152**: 228–234. (Mandibles of *Neos capritermes*)

97. KALSHOVEN, L. G. E. (1959) *Insectes soc.* **6**: 231–242. (Colonie. of *Neotermes*)

98. KARLSON, P., LÜSCHER, M., HUMMEL, H. (1968) *J. Insect Physiol.* **14**: 1763–1772. (Extraction and testing of *Zootermopsis* trail pheromone)

99. KENNEDY, J. S. (1967) in *Insects and Physiology*, Ed. Beament and Treherne, Edinburgh and London. (Insect behaviour as physiology)

100. KÖNIG, J. G. (1779) *Besch. Berlin Ges, naturf. Freunde* **4**: 1–28. (Early account of termites)

101. LEBRUN, D. (1967) *Bull. biol. Fr. Belg.* **101**: 1–87. (Caste determination in *Kalotermes*)

102. LIGHT, S. F. (1929) *Circ. calif, Agr. exp. Station.* **314**. (Termites and termite damage)

103. LIGHT, S. F. (1942) *Q. Rev. Biol.* **17**: 312–326. (Caste determination in social insects)

104. LIGHT, S. F. (1943) *Q. Rev. Biol.* **18**: 46–63. (Continuation)

105. LIGHT, S. F. (1944) *Univ. Calif. Publs Zool.* **43**: 413–454. (Production of neotenics in *Zootermopsis*)

106. LUBBOCK, J. (1882) *Ants, Bees, and Wasps.* London

107. LÜSCHER, M. (1951) *Acta Tropica* **8**: 36–43. (Swarming and colony foundation of African termites)

108. LÜSCHER, M. (1951) *Nature, Lond.* **167**: 34–35. (Fungus gardens)

109. LÜSCHER, M. (1952) *Z. vergl. Physiol.* **34**: 123–141. (Control of neotenics in *Kalotermes*)

110. LÜSCHER, M. (1955) *Acta Tropica* **12**: 289–307. (Air circulation in *Macrotermes* mounds)

111. LÜSCHER, M. (1960) *Ann. N.Y. Acad. Sci.* **89**: 549–563. (Caste differentiation in termites)

112. LÜSCHER, M. (1961) *Symp. R. ent. Soc. Lond.* **1**: 57–67. (Caste determination in termites—review)

113. LÜSCHER, M. (1964) *Insectes soc.* **11**: 79–90. (Sex-specific pheromones in *Kalotermes*)

114. LÜSCHER, M. (1961) *Scient. Am.* **205**: 138–145. (Air-conditioned termite nests)

115. LÜSCHER, M., MÜLLER, B. (1960) *Naturwissenschaften* **21**: 503. (Trail pheromone of *Zootermopsis*)

116. LÜSCHER, M., SPRINGHETTI, A. (1960) *J. Insect Physiol.* **5**: 190–212. (Caste influenced by gland implantation)

117. MACHADO, A. DE B. (1959) *Proc. int. Congr. zool.* **15**: 205–207. (Termite nest structure and systematics)

118. MAETERLINCK, M. (1927) *The Life of the White Ant.* London

119. MARAIS, E. N. (1937) *The Soul of the White Ant.* London

120. MASCHWITZ, U. (1966) *Z. vergl. Physiol.* **53**: 228–252. (Secretions of wasp larvae)

121. MATHOT, G. (1964) In *Études sur les Termites Africains*, Ed. Bouillon. Leopoldville (UNESCO). (Rhythm of nutrition of *Cubitermes*)

122. MATSUMARA, F., COPPEL, H. C., TAI, A. (1968) *Nature, Lond.* **219**: 963–964. (Trail pheromone of *Reticulitermes*)

123. MEDAWAR, P. B. (1969) *Encounter* **32**: 15–23. (Science and literature)

124. MOORE, B. P. (1966) *Nature, Lond.* **211**: 746. (Trail pheromones)

125. MOORE, B. P. (1968) *J. Insect. Physiol.* **14**: 33–40. (Cephalic gland secretion)

126. MOORE, B. P. (1968) *J. Insect Physiol.* **14**: 33–40. (Chemistry of soldier secretions)

127. MYERS, J. G. (1938) *Proc. R. ent. Soc. Lond.* (*A*) **13**: 7–8. (Epigamic behaviour of *Microtermes*)

128. NEL, J. C. C. (1968) *Insectes Soc.* **15**: 145–156. (Aggressive behaviour of harvester termites)

129. NOIROT, C. (1955) *Annls. Sci. nat.* (*Zool.*) **11**: 399–595. (Caste development in the Termitidae)

130. NOIROT, C. (1959) *Insectes soc.* **6**: 259–268. (Nests of *Globitermes*)

131. NOIROT, C. (1959) *Annls. Soc. r. zool. belge* **89**: 151–159. (Ecology of termites)

References 143

132. NOIROT, C., NOIROT-TIMOTHÉE C., (1962) *Symposia Genetica et biol. it.* **11**: 180–188. (Reconstruction of nest in *Cubitermes fungifaber*)

133. PASTEELS, J. M. (1965) *Biologica Gabonica, Perigueux* **1**: 191–205. (Polyethism in *Nasutitermes*)

134. REGNIER, F. E., WILSON, E. O. (1968) *J. Insect Physiol.* **14**: 995–1013. (Alarm heromones of ants)

135. RICHARD, G. (1953) *Annls Sci. nat.* (*Zool*) **14**: 415–421. (Sense-organs and swarming)

136. RICHARD, G. (1956) *J. Psychol. norm. path.*: 502–527. (Geotaxis in *Kalotermes*)

137. RICHARD, G. (1957) *Insectes Soc.* **4**: 107–111. (Antennal sensilla of *Kalotermes*)

138. ROEDER, K. D. (1963) *Nerve Cells and Insect Behaviour.* Harvard

139. ROMANES, G. J. (1883) *Animal Intelligence.* London

140. RUELLE, J. E. (1964) In *Études sur les Termites Africains*, Ed. Bouillon. Leopoldville (UNESCO). (Swarming of *Macrotermes*, regulation of nest climate (2 papers))

141. RUPPLI, E., LÜSCHER, M. (1964) *Revue suisse Zool.* **71**: 626–631. (Elimination of neotenics)

142. SANDS, W. A. (1961) *Entomologia exp. appl.* **4**: 277–288. (Foraging habits of *Trinervitermes*)

143. SANDS, W. A. (1965) *J. Anim. Ecol.* **34**: 557–571. (Distribution of *Trinervitermes* in W. Africa)

144. SANDS, W. A. (1965) *Insectes soc.* **12**: 117–130. (Flight and colony foundation in *Trinervitermes*)

145.* SCHMIDT, H. (Ed.) (1955) *Die Termiten, ihre Erkennungsmerkmale und wirtschaftliche Bedeutung.* Leipzig.

146. SCHMIDT, R. S. (1955) *Behaviour* **8**: 344–356. (*Apicotermes* nests)

147. SCHMIDT, R. S. (1955) *Evolution, Lancaster, Pa.* **9**: 157–181. (Evolution of *Apicotermes* nests)

148. SCHMIDT, R. S. (1958) *Behaviour* **12**: 76–94. (Nest of *Apicotermes trägrådhi*)

149. SCHNEIRLA, T. C. (1964) In *Principles of Animal Psychology*, Ed. Maier and Schneirla. New York. (Approach/withdrawal theory)

150. SCHNEIRLA, T. C. (1965) In *Advances in the Study of Behaviour* **1**: 1–125. (Approach/withdrawal theory)

151.* SKAIFE, S. H. (1955) *Dwellers in Darkness.* London

152. SMEATHMAN, H. (1781) *Phil. Trans. R. Soc. Ser. B*: **71**: 139–192. (Early account of African termites)

153.* SNYDER, T. E. (1935) *Our Enemy the Termite.* New York

154. SNYDER, T. E. (1956) *Smithson. misc. Collns. 130.* (Bibliography of termites until 1954)

155. SNYDER, T. E. (1961) *Smithson, misc. Collns. 143:* no. 3. (Bibliography of termites, 1954–1960)

155b. SNYDER, T. E. (1968) *Smithson, misc. Collins.* **152:** no. 3 (Bibliography of termites, 1961–1965)

156. STUART, A. M. (1961) *Nature, Lond.* **189:** 419 (Pheromone. trails of termites)

157. STUART, A. M. (1964) *Proc. zool. Soc. Lond.* **143:** 43–52. (Structure of sternal gland of *Zootermopsis*)

158. STUART, A. M., SATIR, P. (1968) *J. Cell. Biol.* **36:** 527–549. (Structure of sternal gland of *Zootermopsis*)

159. VERRON, H. (1963) *Insectes soc.* **10:** 167–184. (Chemical basis of social attraction)

160. VERRON, H., BARBIER, M. (1962) *C. r. hebd. Séanc. Acad. Sci. Paris* **254:** 4089–4091. (Chemical attractant for termites)

161. WATSON, J. P. (1967) *J. Ecol.* **55:** 663–665. (Termite mound dated to iron age)

162. WEESNER, F. M. (1956) *Univ. Calif. Publs Zool.* **61:** 253–306. (Colony foundation in *Reticulitermes*)

163.* WEESNER, F. M. (1960) *A. Rev. Ent.* **5:** 153–170. (Evolution and biology of termites—review)

164. WEIDNER, H. (1955) In *Die Termiten,* Ed. Schmidt. Leipzig.

165. WHEELER, W. M. (1911) *J. Morph.* **22:** 307–325. (Superorganism theory)

166. WILKINSON, W. (1962) *Bull. ent. Res.* **55:** 265–286. (Flight and colony foundation in *Cryptotermes*)

167. WILLIAMS, R. M. C. (1959) *Insectes soc.* **6:** 203–218 .(Swarming of *Cubitermes*)

INDEX

Nnumbers in bold type refer to line-drawings